FIGURES/FACES

FIGURES/

A Sketcher's

Hugh

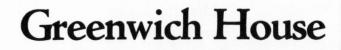

Greenwich House

FACES

Handbook

Laidman

Distributed by
Crown Publishers, Inc.   New York

Copyright © 1979 by Hugh Laidman

This 1983 edition is published by Greenwich House,
a division of Arlington House, Inc.,
distributed by Crown Publishers, Inc.,
by arrangement with The Viking Press

Manufactured in the United States of America

Library of Congress Cataloging in Publication Data

Laidman, Hugh.
   Figures/faces.

   Reprint. Originally published: New York : Viking Press,
1979. (A Studio book)
   1. Human figure in art.   2. Face in art.   3. Drawing–
Technique.   I. Title.
NC765.L28   1983   743′.4   82-11729

ISBN: 0-517-392194

h g f e d c b a

This book is for Betty with love

My warm thanks to the models, who, through the years, have shivered or perspired in drafty studios, to Jean Caffrey, R.N., and Robert Schultz, M.D., who gave of their expertise, and to Virginia Cornwall, who gave of her time and good thoughts.

CONTENTS

Sketches at a ballet class, Chautauqua Institute.
Hugh Laidman, 1971.

INTRODUCTION

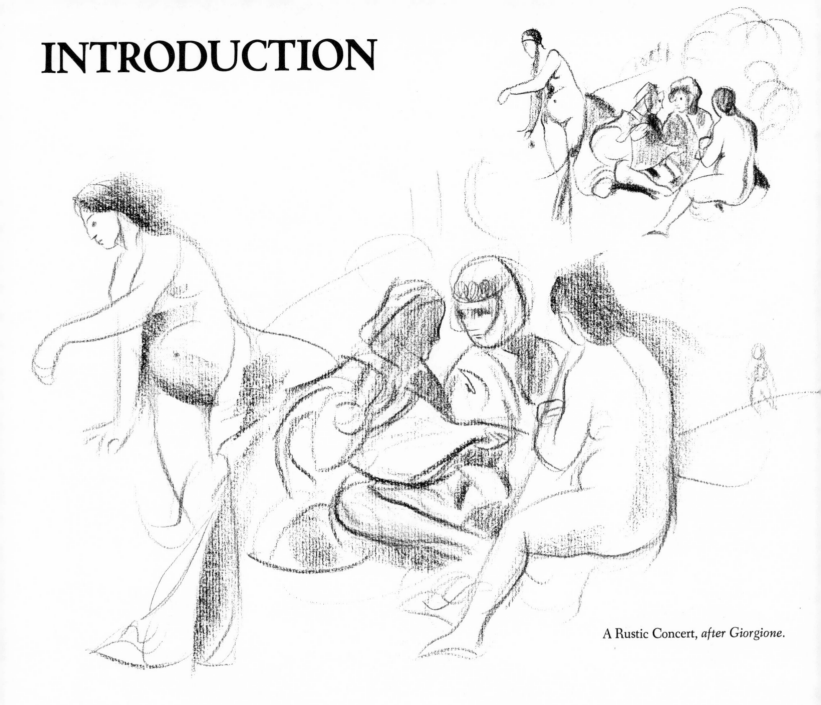

A Rustic Concert, *after Giorgione.*

Figure drawing is drawing the male or female figure unclothed. To draw the clothed figure with any degree of authority demands a knowledge of what goes on beneath the clothes. Some of the best figure artists are fashion artists whose work is to create drawings that sell clothes. Whatever the artist's specialty, illustration or design, he or she is the better for a knowledge of figure drawing.

Figure drawing is not only a form of study that precedes drawing the clothed figure. Frequently it can be appealing in its own right. Goya painted two *Majas,* one clothed, one in the altogether. Of the two, the unclothed is the most remembered.

Thus Goya's posthumous fame as an artist-libertine, although church records show him indulging in periods of fervent religious devotion.

Few life drawings endure to become examples of great art. (The term "life drawing" applies to drawing nudes in art classes, mainly in college, but occasionally in high school.) Calamitous as most of these early attempts are, making them serves to give artists a solid foundation for all drawing. Fortunately most life studies do not survive past their creator's graduation from art school.

I have drawn half a dozen sketches from the works of the old masters. This is a fine method of study, and not a suggestion to slavishly copy paintings. The idea is to create your idea of what the early sketches of these great works may have looked like. It is meaningless to merely copy anything. Studying, accompanied by analytical sketching, is helpful. You won't be the first to use this method of learning. The great artist Manet, inspired by *A Rustic Concert,* went on to make a fairly close interpretation that is as famous today as the original. All I intend you to do is study the works of some of the past masters by making quick sketches.

In your search for models you will likely encounter more re-sistance to posing in the nude from men than from women; more from underachievers than from Phi Beta Kappas of either sex. It is usually vanity, not modesty, that triggers the balk at posing. The guy knows that his clothes hide a spare tire . . . the lady might like a little more time at exercise class before stepping on the model stand.

Generally a group of artists can locate and pay for a model for weekday evenings or Saturday afternoons. Relatives, friends, and most especially other artists are the best source of non-professional model supply, short of joining a nudist club. The simple fact is that the relative temperature of the studio has most to do with the willingness of people to pose as life models. When the artists are comfortable, the model is freezing.

When no nude model is around, draw the clothed model (re-ferred to in art circles as "draped"). If you have no model, practice drawing from memory.

Use your modest friends in bathing suits. Cut action figures from newspapers and magazines, try to draw the body under-neath, squint your eyes and do quick sketches. Draw from statues in an art museum. Use your mirror.

The student, in drawing the figure, is faced with seemingly contradictory aims. On the one hand he is attempting to draw a recognizable figure, on the other he wishes to avoid the dead, mechanical look. To further confuse the issue, in today's aesthetic climate things are seldom what they seem. Ingenious imitation, trickery, and accident are frequently substituted for creative ability. In the early stages of figure drawing, a heavy emphasis will be upon drawing what you see.

In the beginning, as you draw what you see before you, you will stress the things you wish to stress and eliminate what you feel should be eliminated. As you draw, you will gravitate around a fixed point. You will approach the problem of learning to draw the figure in many positions and from many directions. You will draw in many techniques. One or more of the ways may appeal.

Somehow you must approach both the aesthetics of drawing and the logic of drawing at one and the same time. In your early figure drawings you will concentrate on construction and form. At first you will be concerned mainly with how to get lines and tones in such relationship, one to the other, that the viewer can identify what you have drawn. The aesthetics of the drawings may become apparent even before you have mastered the mechanics. Your batting average will go up once you have mastered the tools, materials, and a few fundamentals. Once you can put the line or tone on the paper where you want the line or tone to be, then you can say to the viewer, "That is what I meant to say."

Diana Quitting Her Bath with One of Her Attendants,
after Boucher.

11

Psyche and Cupid, *after Gérard.*

Over the years the majority of those who boasted of any degree of art awareness approached art in the belief that the artist had a predetermined conception of any work he had in the planning stage. This is in direct contrast to a currently popular trend of public art appreciation in which the artist, after completing his drawing, waits for the critics to tell him what he, the artist, had in mind.

The established theory of fine art distinguishes art from nature by saying that man premeditates and fabricates art while nature goes on with no help from him. A robin's song, however beautiful, is instinctive rather than fine art. To be considered an artist, from the time of the very first stirrings of prehistoric man, he had to make something, even if it was only for himself. The art of drawing is the art of objective completion, as contrasted with dance and music, which emphasize the influence of interpretation.

While theory is no substitute for talent, certain theory in practice might uncover dormant talent or develop visible talent. By the same thinking, some theory put into practice might stifle potential talent for all time.

When the student looks at his latest creation and thinks privately that it is like nothing else, he must not be discouraged. As Sir C. J. Holmes says in *Notes on the Science of Picture Making*, "All great art, being emphatically personal, is accompanied by variation from previously existing standards." All great artists are pioneers possessing the characteristics that lead to their being almost adamantly original.

The very best way to learn how to draw is by drawing. An excellent practice to help understand and retain what I say in this book is that of taking little graphic notes—making miniature "thumbnail" sketches.

The person who would learn something from this or any book must *think* about what he is doing.

Most artists find it difficult to speak or observe without sketching. The casual observer interprets the action as doodling. Nineteen out of twenty fine or commercial artists, architects, or designers do this. Sculptors carry the practice to an extreme, doodling on anything at hand—napkins, tablecloths, parts of humans. Before you read another word, get a pad, pencil, a felt-tip or other pen, and begin your miniature, graphic notes.

Jupiter and Antiope, *after Correggio.*

In a study of any of the fine arts, doing something other than reading, listening, or looking becomes a vital part of the learning process. You're not going to get the first chair in the Philadelphia Symphony by reading about how to play the French horn. You'll never make prima ballerina by looking at old ballet movies. You're not going to become the great American novelist by speed-reading *Tom Sawyer*. Remember that superintelligence is no prerequisite of the accomplished artist. It is an historical fact that many of the greatest figure artists were intellectual slobs and, working as they did in charcoal, most had dirty fingernails.

There are a number of approaches to beginning a drawing. The Oriental approach is one of concentrating on a blank drawing surface and attempting to visualize the finished product. The amateur, and sometimes Western, approach is quite the opposite—start work on the drawing and try to salvage what you can later.

Smudge drawing.

Construction drawing.

It is not suggested that Eastern art is therefore superior to Western art, but rather that time spent thinking about what you intend to draw should precede drawing. In practice, neither of these approaches to drawing is limited to citizens of either East or West.

Almost all poor drawings are inferior because the artist spent more time drawing than thinking about what he was drawing. The artist's relative IQ is not as important to the

Outline drawing.

The process really doesn't work that way. In this book we will try a variety of learning approaches that have worked for artists throughout the years, including contour drawing, outline drawing, gesture drawing, sustained drawing, forced edge drawing, action drawing, line drawing, and dynamic symmetry.

In action study, the student is involved not so much with the physical outline as with the apparent motion and feel of the figure. If the student begins to scribble aimlessly without concentrating on his interpretation of the model, his work will result in a meaningless jumble of lines.

If, on the other hand, the student observes and thinks about what the model is doing, this contemplation will take effect in a more meaningful drawing. The more the student knows about the subject the better chance he has of making a convincing drawing. That's the reason we study the bones, the muscles, and the basic shapes.

In "contour" drawing, the artist, in certain schools of teaching, imagines that his pencil or whatever is actually touching the outline of the model, and he slowly follows the contour without looking at his drawing.

quality of his work as is his relative use of his intelligence. Even if an artist is a whiz at intelligence tests, his finished drawings will not necessarily be any better than those of a two-year-old. It is the intensity of concentration and feeling that will determine the final result. Creativity has little if anything to do with IQ.

In the world of the sculptor there is a method called "taille direct," which means to start right in hacking the marble without benefit of preliminary modeling. Two fellows who could get away with this were Michelangelo and Rodin, and Michelangelo advised against it.

The lesson then is: Think about the line or tone before you put it on the paper.

It is an accepted belief that almost anyone, artist or non-artist, can spot the slightest inaccuracy in a drawing of the human figure. It follows that if any of these observers can see that a nose is off center, or that one leg is longer than the other, then the artist, with a fresh eye, can certainly correct the drawing with no help from the audience.

Drawing with side of pastel stick.

The early results of this exercise will be anyone's guess. Done with little or no direction, it can be an aimless parlor game. With concentration, it becomes a valuable exercise.

It is easy for the student to find himself mired in semantics. One teacher may insist that quick sketching is of little to no value in learning to draw, but by the substitution of the word "study" for "sketch," everything is back on stream. The constant is still that of an intelligent thinking approach to fast drawing, whatever we call it.

The action sketch may concentrate on the process of changing form. More than likely, the elements of form and mass will be secondary to the lines. This is not to suggest that a painstakingly finished drawing cannot express action. It can, but it is less likely to.

Forced edge drawings.

Contour drawing.

All these approaches to drawing are important. Each reinforces the next. The more lines, tones, and detail you introduce into a drawing, the more chances you take of spoiling the finished work.

Rapid sketching from poses limited to one to five minutes, or even poses in which the model changes positions without pause, are excellent exercises to force the student to observe. Following the principle that learning to see and retain is a good part of becoming skilled at drawing anything, try a number of approaches to this end.

Abstain from drawing while the model poses. Once the model has stopped posing, proceed to draw from memory.

Observe one view of the model and draw another. Before the model changes position, go around to the other side, the side which you have imagined. See how close your drawing is to what, while standing in another spot, you imagined the model would look like.

The artist first mentally constructs or divides or re-creates the figure. He thinks in terms of mass, planes, and line prior to putting anything on paper. No two people draw exactly alike and, to a greater or lesser degree, this will show in the relative strength or frailty of the drawing. One drawing may be composed of beautiful lines; the other, of ugly scrawls.

The traditional and probably the most enjoyable way to develop memory is by constantly sketching everything and everyone you see. In sports, ofttimes an identical action is repeated again and again, offering an excellent opportunity for sketching practice.

No matter what you are drawing, it will be best to concentrate mainly on the action. Sometimes you see reproductions of very finished drawings purported to have been sketched on the spot. Chances are the idea was generated on the spot; possibly, action lines and the roughest of figures were conceived at that moment. It is more than likely, however, that photos were taken and that final sketches you are viewing were made from a combination of this reference material. (Photographs used in the completion of drawings are always referred to as reference material by fine artists and as scrap by commercial artists and illustrators.)

Had Leonardo da Vinci and Michelangelo had available to them our contemporary knowledge of photography, fast lenses, and faster film, along with color and projection, they might very well have produced even greater masterpieces. On the other hand, had they used them wrongly, as many do today, we probably would never have heard of them.

17

The camera can be used for study and as an aid in drawing, but its continual use is dangerous. The photograph can become a crutch for the lazy artist, a crutch he, too late, discovers he cannot toss away.

Years ago when I was a student of illustration at Pratt Institute, four of us were invited to attend a rather festive party at the Illustrators' Club. At the time, the tide had not yet started to run out on the world of fine illustrations, and illustrators were the idols of every art student, even those who had decided to opt for fine art as a career. There were many illustrators, though, aware of the handwriting on the wall, who were taking the first steps toward creating paintings suitable for framing. None of the four select embryo illustrators picked to attend the cocktail party had an inkling that the world of the illustrator was about to collapse. It soon suffered several knockout punches: first, hard times, where photographs could be used for less money than drawings. Then World War II, which depleted the ranks of practicing illustrators, and finally, the post-war period, which saw the demise of one slick magazine after another, along with all the illustrated pulps.

The four of us went to the Illustrators' party. Everyone was there, including a beautiful (and famous) singer in a gorgeous black and white evening gown. I don't know why, or whether things were so planned, but at some time in the evening she, in her lovely gown, posed for the illustrators. The resulting drawings were at best disappointing. Those illustrators who drew made a series of tiny, almost plaintive scratches. A popular cartoonist of the time was an exception. His daily work was that of large drawings, cartoons to be sure, in a technique that just lent itself to sketching from the live model. I seem to recollect that he left with the lady. . . .

The ones who came up looking like roses were we four kids. Fresh from three years of day-in, day-out sketching from the model, with never a hint of a photograph, we were, one might say, in training. It's very likely that most of the illustrators there could have returned to their past expertise in drawing from the live model in short order, but a career of working from photographs had had its toll.

Soon most of the great illustrators who attended the party were gone—gone to wherever illustrators go when the illustrating business dries up. I vowed never to get too tied into the photograph bit.

PART I / FIGURES

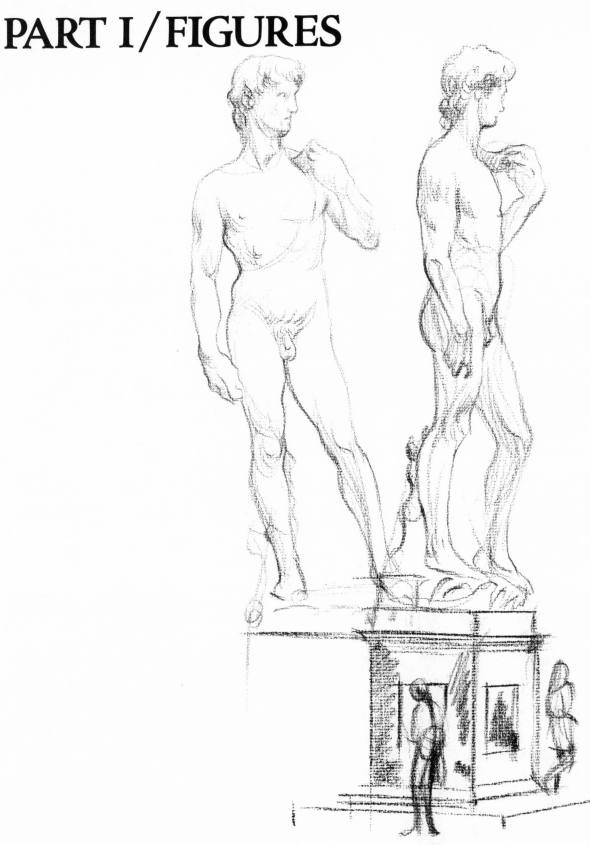

I am sketching Michelangelo's *David* in the Florence Accademia. A busload of German tourists crowds through. The guard asks me to move. I take another position out of the traffic pattern. For the first time I realize how large *David* is. I draw the little girl at the foot of the pediment. I remember the story my old German art instructor told me—the top of *David*'s head is still unfinished. . . . I think of all the work I've left un-

done and feel a little closer to Michelangelo. I think, as I draw, I can see the sculptor chipping away.

Because I have been drawing what I have been seeing and thinking about what I have been drawing, my impression of *David* may be closer to indelible than the impressions of most of those German tourists.

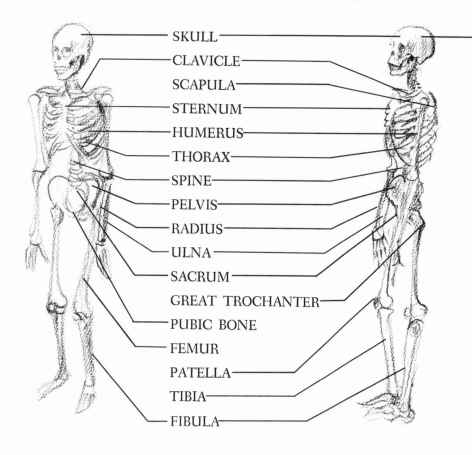

SKULL
CLAVICLE
SCAPULA
STERNUM
HUMERUS
THORAX
SPINE
PELVIS
RADIUS
ULNA
SACRUM
GREAT TROCHANTER
PUBIC BONE
FEMUR
PATELLA
TIBIA
FIBULA

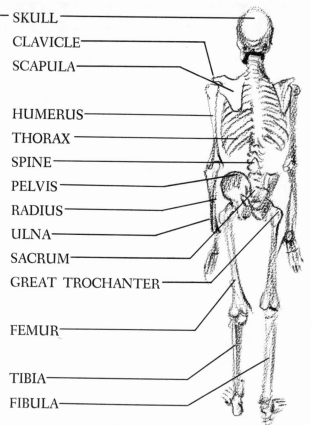

SKULL
CLAVICLE
SCAPULA

HUMERUS
THORAX
SPINE
PELVIS
RADIUS
ULNA
SACRUM
GREAT TROCHANTER

FEMUR

TIBIA
FIBULA

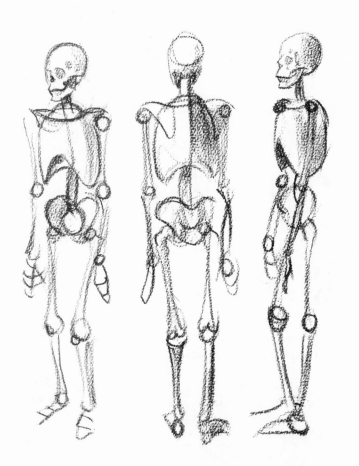

Bones

Above we have identified the major bones. It is not necessary to remember all the names, but it helps to be familiar enough with them for easy reference in the beginning. In the study of the bones, the framework of the figure, we begin to comprehend the possible degree or limit of motion of the parts of the human structure.

We can simplify the skeleton for the sake of drawing to the elements shown in the three views on the left.

At the top of page 21 are illustrations of the three main parts of the skeleton. The backbone, a series of tiny interlocked bones, connects the three parts. The important thing for the artist to remember is that the spine is a flexible column to which the three main inflexible parts are attached. The movement of these parts in relation to one another is in direct relation to the degree of flexibility of this connecting column.

The lower jaw moves in the skull, the pelvic girdle does change during childbirth, but fundamentally these three masses are static shapes.

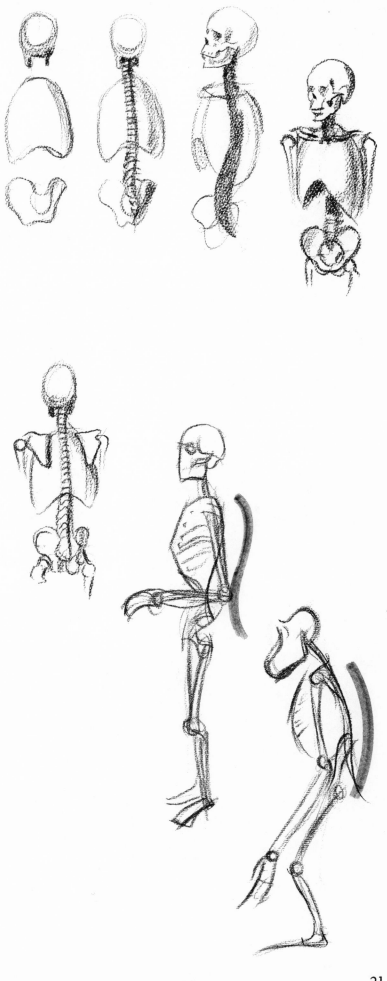

Bearing in mind that the bones of most mammals, including the human, would fall into an untidy pile but for the fact that they are tied neatly together by an amazing structure of tendons and muscles, we will attempt a simplification of the human anatomy.

The upper arm bone (humerus) fits into a socket in the scapula, and the scapula in turn works in conjunction with the collarbone (clavicle), completing the collar around the neck. The scapula (shoulder blade) is anything but stationary, joined by clavicles right and left, one for each shoulder blade. The clavicles in turn almost meet at the front of the rib cage (sternum, or breastbone). It is traditional for the instructor to explain that the bone called the clavicle is so named because of its resemblance in shape to an ancient Latin key. This adds a bit of seasoning to an otherwise bland subject. More interesting to the artist is the fact that even in overweight people we can detect the clavicles beneath the skin and muscle.

The upper femur has a ball-like structure that fits into a socket in the pelvis.

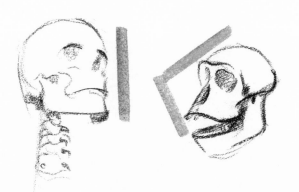

In the human, the spine has an S curve. In the gorilla, another primate, the curve of the spine is that of a C. In the head, the frontal angle of the human is classically a vertical line; that of the gorilla is at a much greater angle.

Using our simplified skeleton of the torso area, make quick sketches of the rib cage, pelvic area, and the skull, connected by the spinal column. The upper section of the rib cage appears wider at the top than it actually is. This is due to the

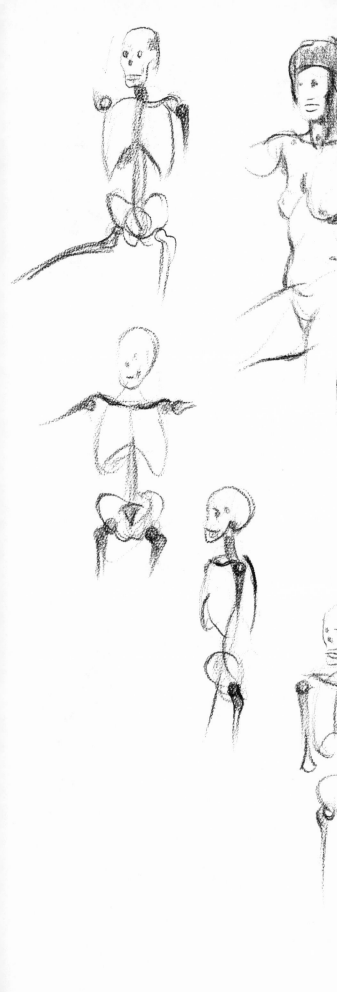

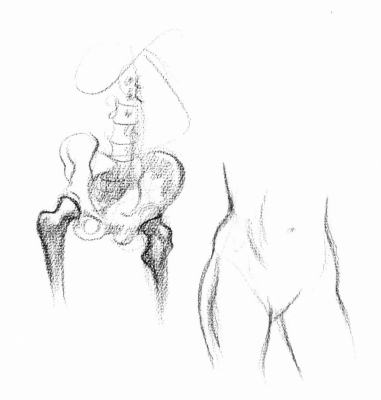

scapulae and collarbones encircling the upper area around the shoulders and neck. The humerus, fitting into this area of scapula and clavicle, helps to give the appearance of a broader upper rib cage. Between the rib cage area and the pelvic area is the epigastrium. Keeping these facts in mind makes it a little simpler to sketch the human figure. Once we have general shapes of these three main masses—skull, rib cage, and pelvic girdle—well in mind, we can attack arms and legs with more assurance.

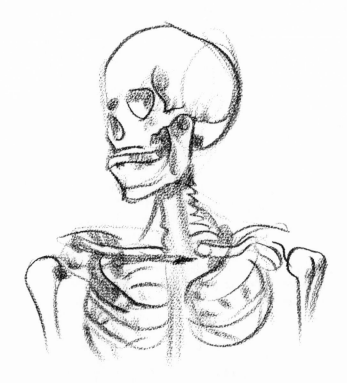

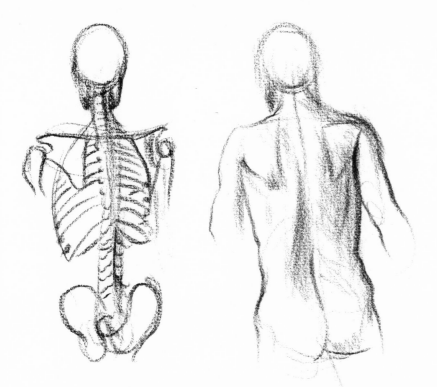

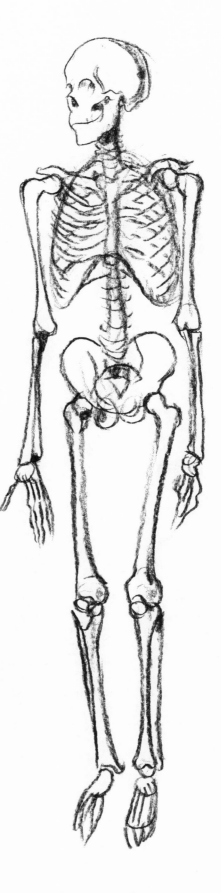

Viewing the figure from the rear, we find a bony area in the vicinity of the small of the back. The bone structure of the arm has certain similarities to that of the leg. The humerus, the single bone of the upper arm, extends to the elbow, at which point two bones, the radius and the ulna, continue to the wrist and hand. In the case of the legs, we have a socket in the pelvis that accepts the femur, which in turn extends to the knee, where we have two bones, the fibula and tibia, extending to the ankle and foot. Draw a couple of thumbnail sketches, first of the skeleton, then of the figure, in similar poses.

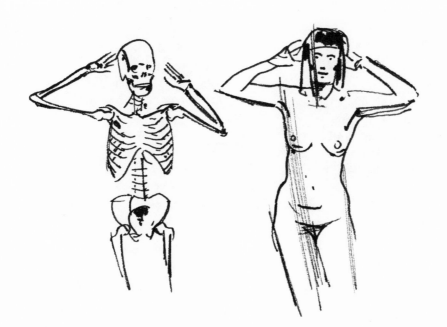

By the time you've study-sketched all my lounging skeletons on these three pages, you'll be better prepared to draw a figure. Make thumbnail sketches of these, bearing in mind what has been said of the skeleton and its functions so far.

There is no formula for producing instant artists. The nearest thing is the simple procedure in which the student *thinks* about every mark he makes on his paper in relation to the subject that he intends to draw and the purpose he had in drawing it in the first place.

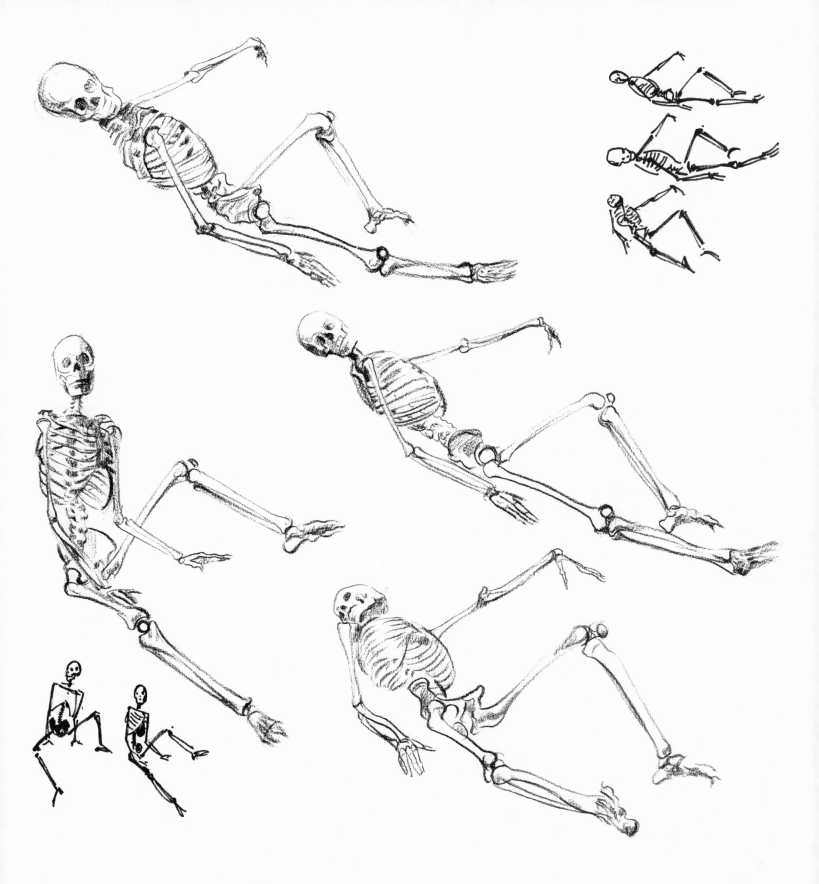

The top three seated skeletons on page 24 are drawn from a skeleton placed in one position. I have merely moved from one vantage point to another to illustrate the variety of drawings possible from a single position of the model. The skeleton at the bottom of page 24 and the lower left skeletons on page 25 are again in one position, but I changed my drawing situation. The remaining drawings on page 25 are of a skeleton lying down on a couch, drawn once again from different viewing points.

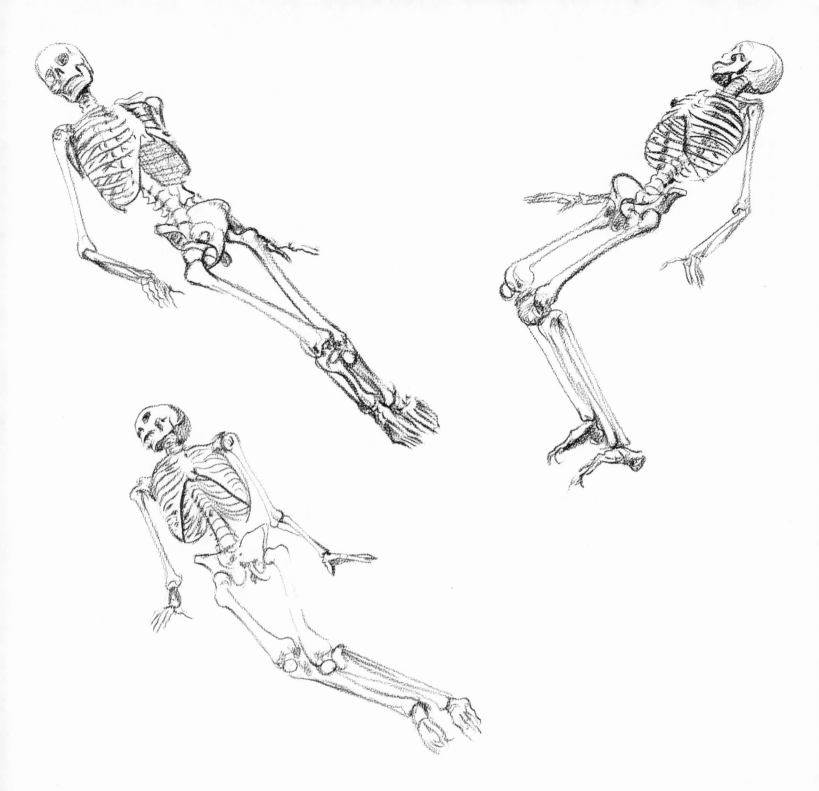

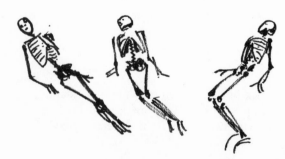

The idea of sketching skeletons in these rather odd positions is to further acquaint the student with the framework of the human figure. Once you have this basic framework well in mind, it will aid you in drawing more convincing figures. At this stage, you need only make little thumbnail sketches, such as those I have included among our drawings of relaxed bones.

Muscles

Once you have become familiar with human bone structure, do a series of sketches from a model. As you draw the figure, preferably from life, try to see where the bones are. Imagine where the rib cage is. Try to locate the scapulae, think of the way the spine bends in the various positions. Later we'll draw figures and fit the skeleton into them, and vice versa. Now, before studying the main muscles, we'll just think about them.

Too great a mastery of anatomical knowledge may make the artist more anatomist than creator. Masters of the past were generally more occupied with anatomy than today's artists. Any comprehensive study of the human form in Renaissance days usually involved a one-on-one relationship with grave robbers, a degree of influence at court, and a strong stomach. Today's student risks only a few pennies' fine for an overdue book at the library in his quest for knowledge. Whatever the source, an intelligent study of the figure is basic to good drawing.

Here and on page 29 I have drawn both sexes in similar positions to point up similarities as well as differences in muscle appearance.

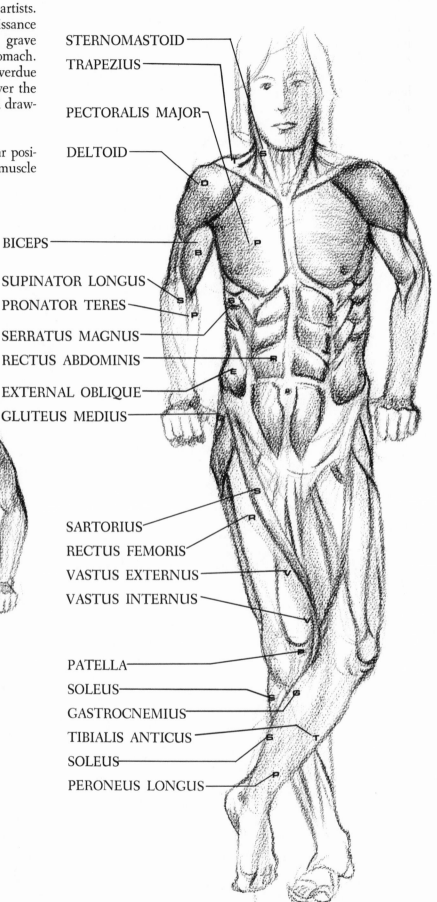

STERNOMASTOID

TRAPEZIUS

PECTORALIS MAJOR

DELTOID

BICEPS

SUPINATOR LONGUS

PRONATOR TERES

SERRATUS MAGNUS

RECTUS ABDOMINIS

EXTERNAL OBLIQUE

GLUTEUS MEDIUS

SARTORIUS

RECTUS FEMORIS

VASTUS EXTERNUS

VASTUS INTERNUS

PATELLA

SOLEUS

GASTROCNEMIUS

TIBIALIS ANTICUS

SOLEUS

PERONEUS LONGUS

The function of the muscles of the body is to supply power for action. They do this in part by contracting, and in so doing, become shorter, harder, broader and more clearly defined. While a given muscle is contracting, a corresponding muscle is extending and pulling against the contracting muscle.

The study of the skeleton is a relatively simple project (with due apologies to orthopedic surgeons). The study of the muscles is far more involved. Quite simply, while bones seldom change their configuration except in the growth process, muscles change shape with any and all action. To further complicate an already difficult subject, there are more muscles than bones. It is small comfort for the figure artist to be told that should his knowledge of the muscles become so thorough that it overshadows the artistic merit of his figure drawing, he has just missed the boat.

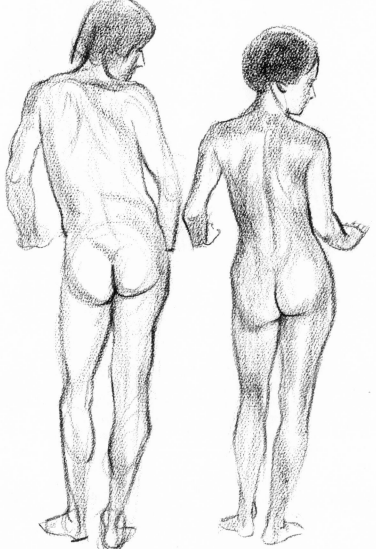

STERNOMASTOID
TRAPEZIUS
DELTOID
TRICEPS

LATISSIMUS DORSI
SUPINATOR LONGUS
EXTENSOR CARPI
ULNARIS

GLUTEUS MEDIUS
GLUTEUS MAXIMUS
SEMITENDINOSUS
BICEPS FEMORIS

SARTORIUS
GASTROCNEMIUS

SOLEUS
ACHILLES TENDON
PERONEUS LONGUS

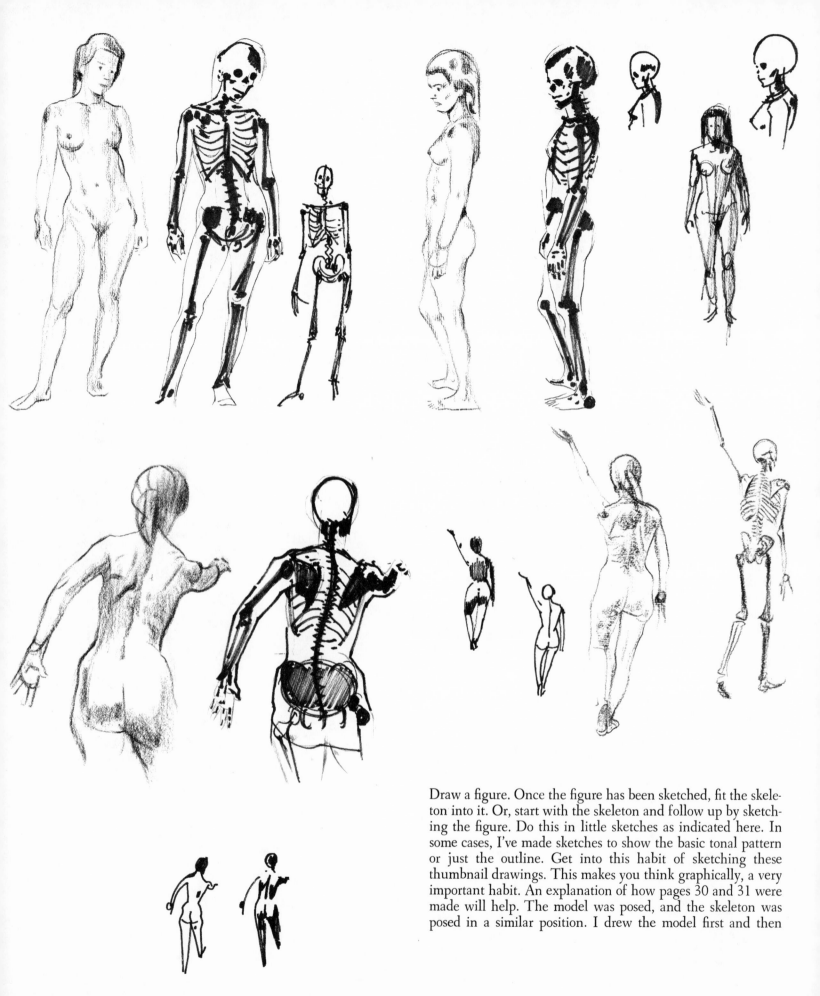

Draw a figure. Once the figure has been sketched, fit the skeleton into it. Or, start with the skeleton and follow up by sketching the figure. Do this in little sketches as indicated here. In some cases, I've made sketches to show the basic tonal pattern or just the outline. Get into this habit of sketching these thumbnail drawings. This makes you think graphically, a very important habit. An explanation of how pages 30 and 31 were made will help. The model was posed, and the skeleton was posed in a similar position. I drew the model first and then

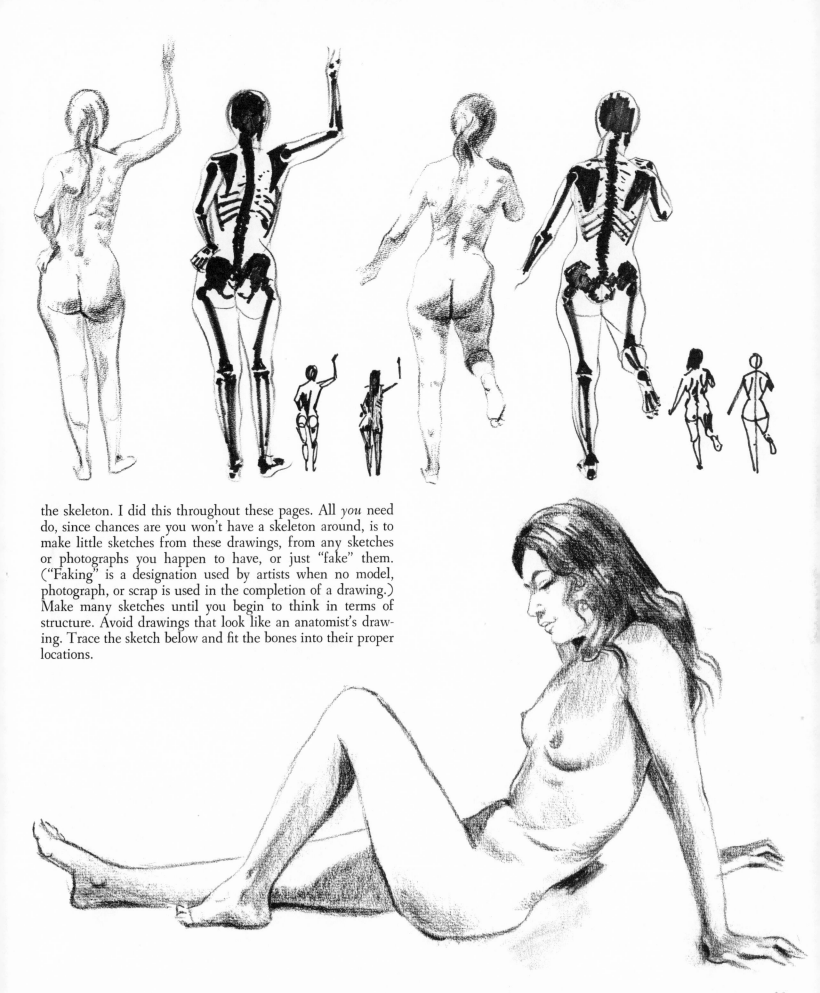

the skeleton. I did this throughout these pages. All *you* need do, since chances are you won't have a skeleton around, is to make little sketches from these drawings, from any sketches or photographs you happen to have, or just "fake" them. ("Faking" is a designation used by artists when no model, photograph, or scrap is used in the completion of a drawing.) Make many sketches until you begin to think in terms of structure. Avoid drawings that look like an anatomist's drawing. Trace the sketch below and fit the bones into their proper locations.

Comparative Structure

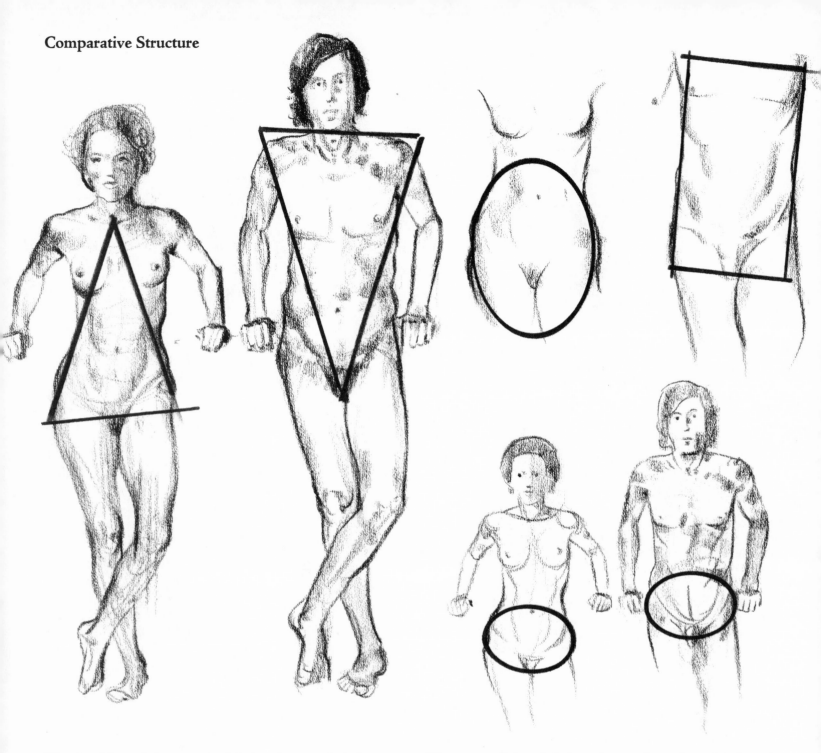

The shoulders of the typical adult female are relatively narrower than those of the adult male. The nipples of the adult male are placed higher on the chest than those of the adult female. The nipples of either sex are not in the center of the breasts, but are toward the outside of the chest area. In the male, the section around the hips seems deeper, bringing the navel relatively higher in the adult male than in the female.

The humerus of the male is relatively longer than that of the female. A long-armed girl will find a sweater from the man's rack more likely to fit. The male's legs are longer, the torso shorter. Should some of these observations seem in conflict one to the next, it merely strengthens the case for simultaneous posing of the two sexes.

The center of the adult is at the crotch, at the pubic bone in the male, just above, in the female. As you study and compare the male and female figures, you will begin to store up your own special observations. No matter how athletic the female, her body does not develop distinct muscles as does the male; no matter how underweight or overweight, she still has a comparatively greater amount of fat over the thighs, the hips, and the buttocks. The buttocks of the male are more rectangular than those of the female, hers being rounder, fleshier, and relatively larger. Despite fads and fashion, this is the basic structure as provided by nature.

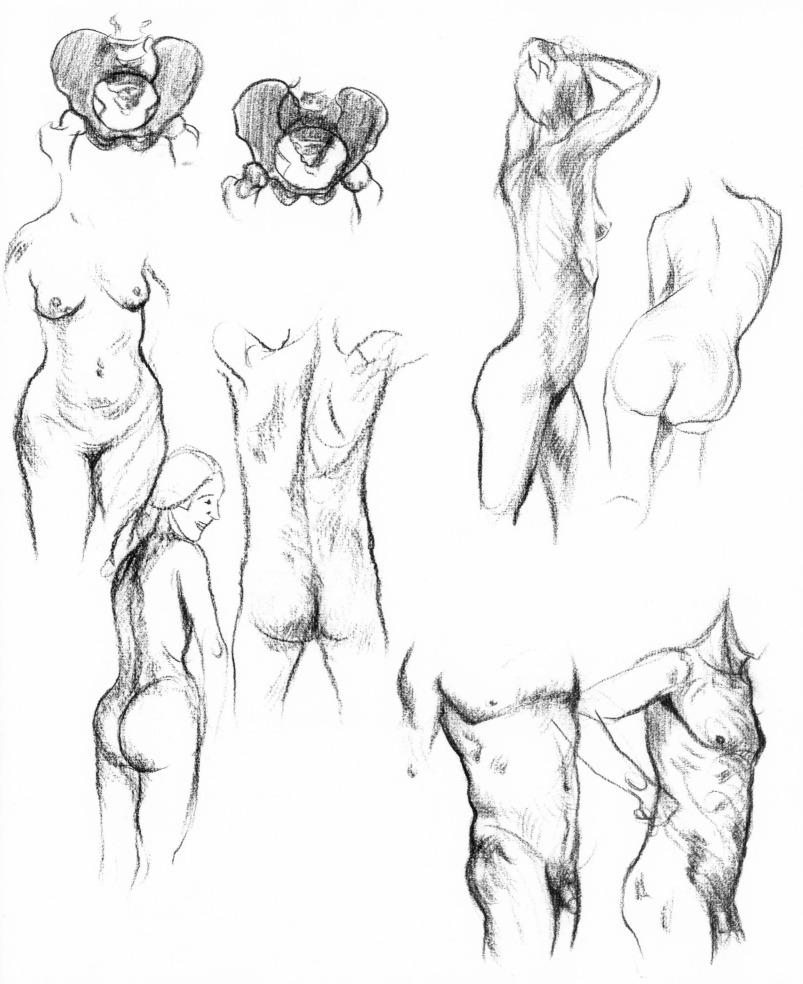

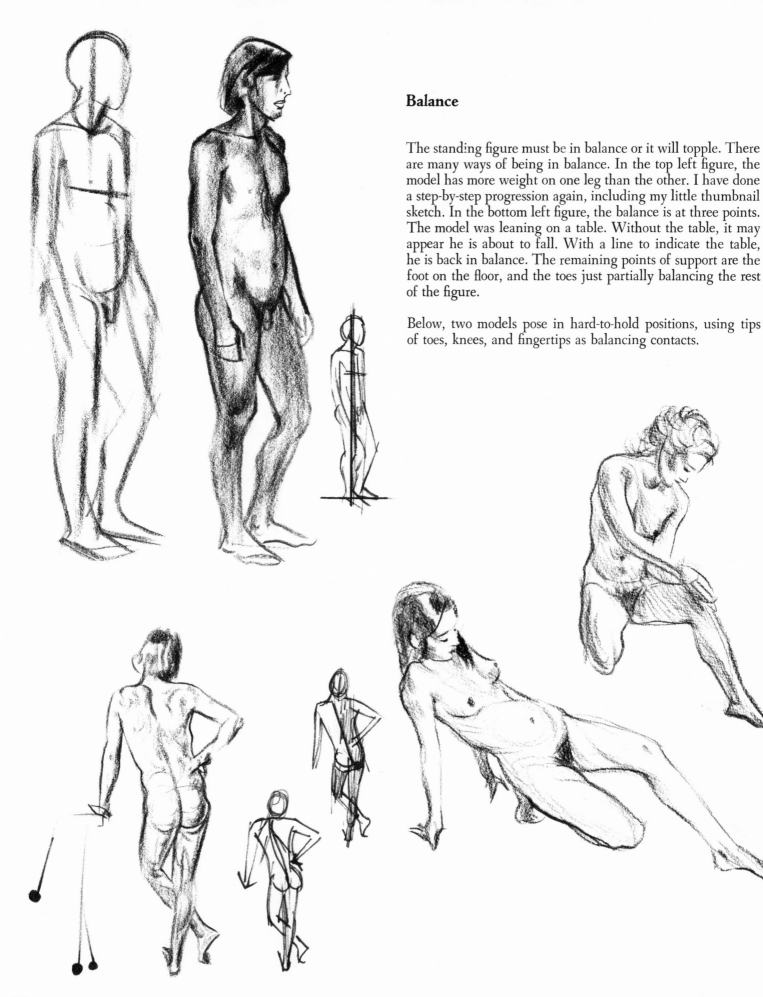

Balance

The standing figure must be in balance or it will topple. There are many ways of being in balance. In the top left figure, the model has more weight on one leg than the other. I have done a step-by-step progression again, including my little thumbnail sketch. In the bottom left figure, the balance is at three points. The model was leaning on a table. Without the table, it may appear he is about to fall. With a line to indicate the table, he is back in balance. The remaining points of support are the foot on the floor, and the toes just partially balancing the rest of the figure.

Below, two models pose in hard-to-hold positions, using tips of toes, knees, and fingertips as balancing contacts.

At the right I have shown a male and a female in similar positions to show the slight difference there is in conformation and attitude. Below them we have a figure kneeling, drawn from two vantage points. Again we have a balance, this time a four-point balance. The arch of the foot forward from toe to heel makes two points. The knee of the other leg and the toes of the foot on the ground make four. Constantly think of balance and weight distribution, as I've shown in my little sketches.

In the sketches below, the feet do the balancing. Remember that each foot has an involved system of balancing: the heel, a forward pad, and five toes.

I have drawn a male model in a similar position to the kneeling female on the preceding page.

If you were doing a portrait, and the model were to get into a position with one leg higher than the other, the final portrait, although showing just neck and head, would have a more relaxed appearance. Photographers know this and will often have a person stand with a foot up on a chair while they are taking a picture of just the head and shoulders. The straight-on pose—standing like a U.S. Marine at attention—is most uninteresting.

Hands

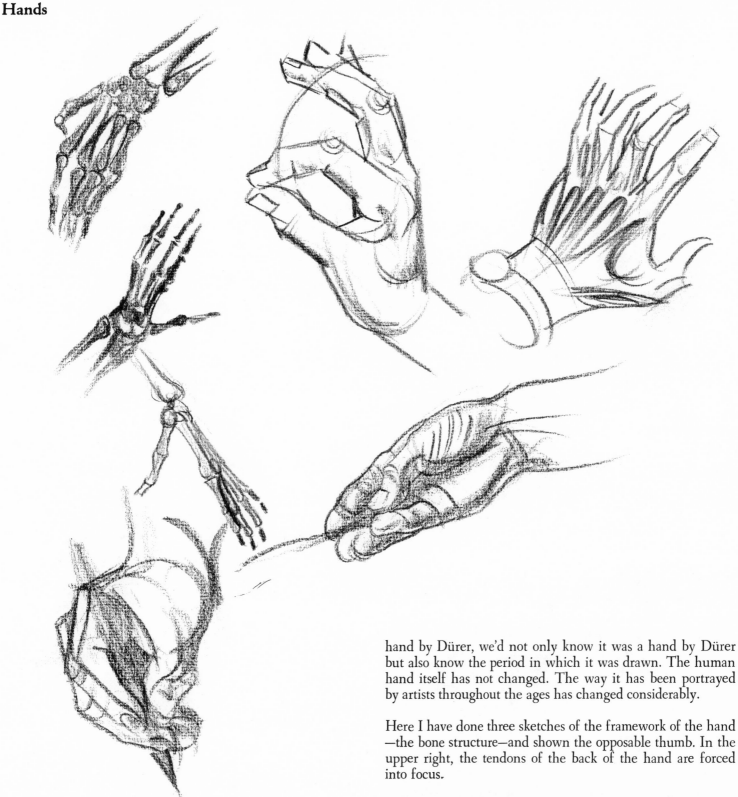

The hand is a most expressive part of the human figure. It can be entreating. It can be threatening. It can be, and frequently is, used as a weapon. It can do many things. Through the years, as different artists have portrayed the hands, each school has been most individual in its interpretation. We can easily recognize a Gothic hand or a Renaissance hand. If it were a hand by Dürer, we'd not only know it was a hand by Dürer but also know the period in which it was drawn. The human hand itself has not changed. The way it has been portrayed by artists throughout the ages has changed considerably.

Here I have done three sketches of the framework of the hand —the bone structure—and shown the opposable thumb. In the upper right, the tendons of the back of the hand are forced into focus.

The happy thing about the study of the hand is that you have built-in models. You can study your own in a mirror or you can look at them in front of you. Keep sketching. Make little sketches and big sketches. Study the hand. You'll find that a good hand in any drawing is going to help carry that drawing. This is the place where many artists fall down. Even non-artists have learned to look to the hands in a drawing when evaluating the relative ability of the artist whose work is under review.

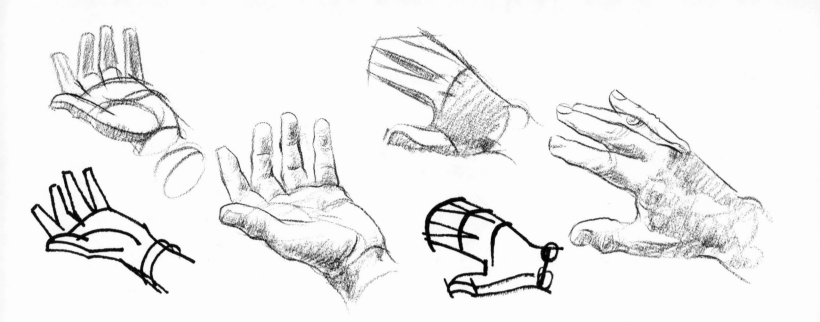

As you draw and redraw your own hands in various positions, you will realize the range of expression that you can achieve. The drawings throughout this section are usually of a pair of hands. In most cases, with a little study, you will observe that I have begun with a line sketch of a given pair of hands, continued into a block structural rendition, and finished with a simple shaded drawing.

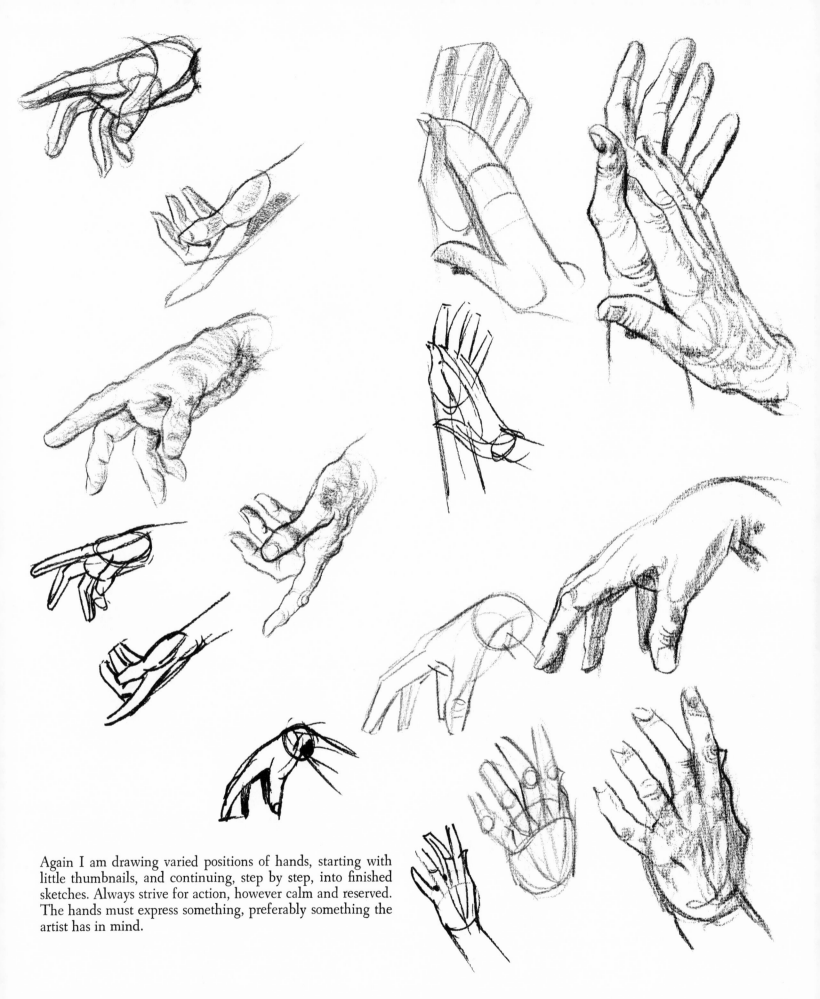

Again I am drawing varied positions of hands, starting with little thumbnails, and continuing, step by step, into finished sketches. Always strive for action, however calm and reserved. The hands must express something, preferably something the artist has in mind.

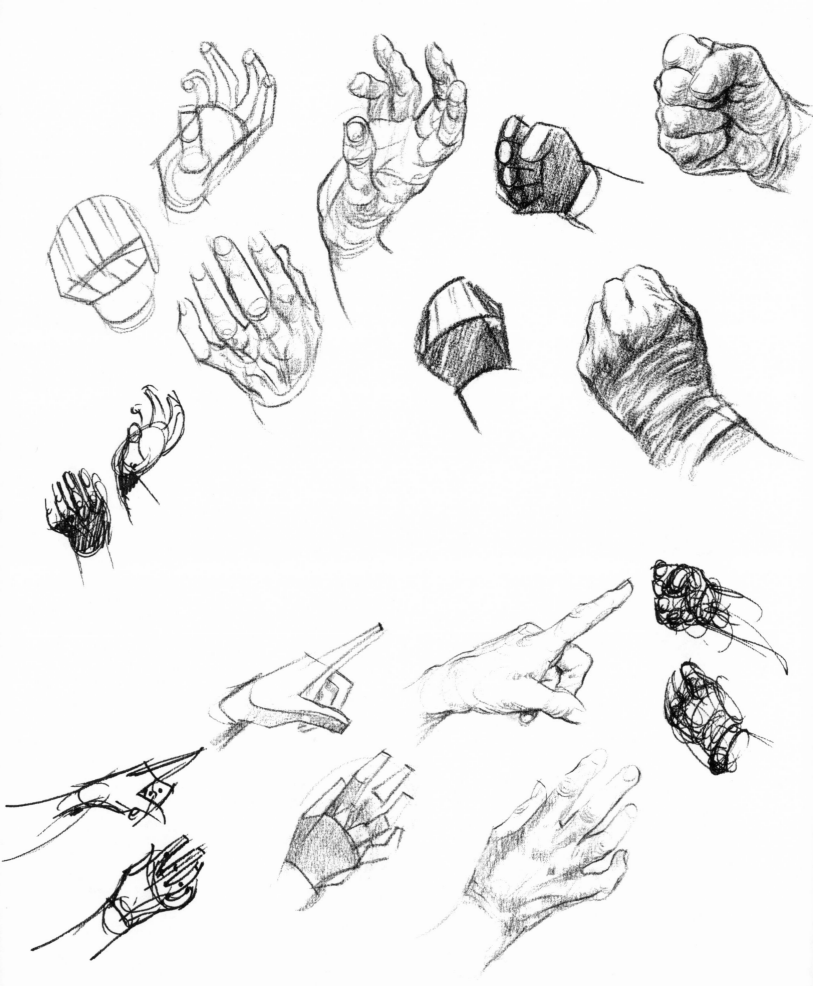

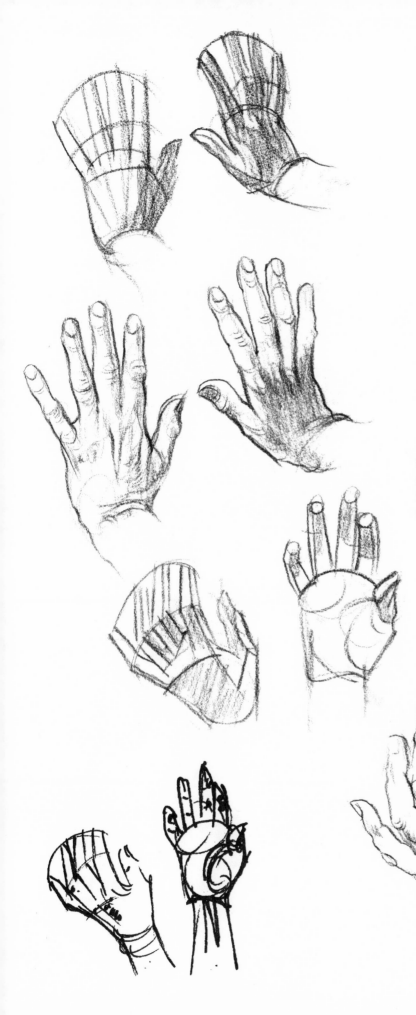

Study the relationship of one finger to the next, all the fingers to the thumb, fingers and thumb to the palm. Study the hand from the back, from the palm. In time you will begin to draw convincing hands.

I have drawn four sketches of the bones of the foot. In my sketch of a pair of feet below the sketches of the bones, note how the ankle bone is lower on the outside of the foot. As you view the inside of one of this same pair, you note the very distinct inside arch of the foot. At the extreme bottom of the page, the flat-footed effect of the outside of the foot is shown. The remaining two feet (not a pair) show the action of a foot running . . . walking.

It would be a good idea to put a mirror in front of you and sketch your own feet in many positions. Study your own feet. You need the mirror because without it you get a limited view. If you can get a model to pose, fine, but it isn't necessary in order to sketch and study the construction and action of the foot.

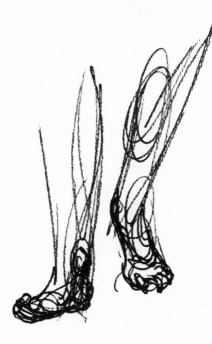

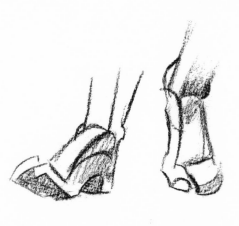

As I draw and redraw my step-by-step procedures on feet, I discover that the early steps are often more convincing than the final drawings. For example: the top right pair of feet are more solid in appearance than the final stage directly below them; the third pair down have more action than the pair on bottom right. This is a most important aspect of all drawing, and serves to point up where the artist's drawing, executed intelligently, differs from the lens of the camera. The artist picks and chooses, he holds back or emphasizes. Only in the hands of an expert can a camera discriminate, and such hands are those of an artist.

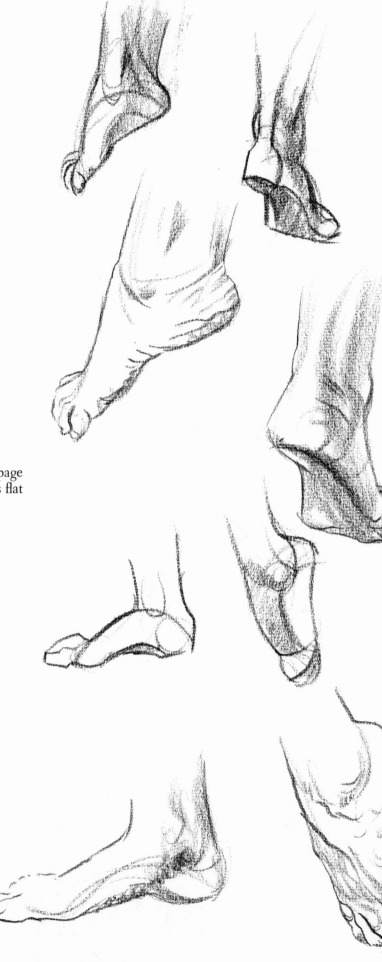

Again we're drawing a pair of feet over and over. On this page we've continued stressing the outside of the foot, which is flat as it contacts the floor, and the inside, which is arched.

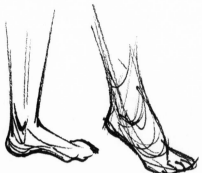

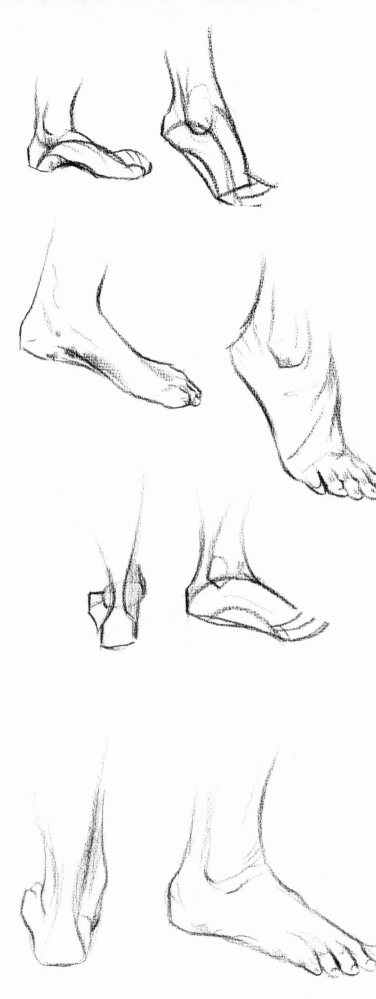

In summing up, the foot is a weight-bearing device. The arch between heel and big toe becomes less as we progress to the outside of the foot. Finally, on the outside of the foot, there is a flat surface from little toe to heel. The distance from the big

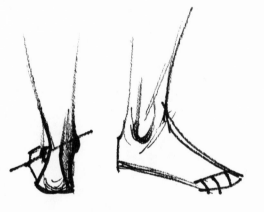

toe to the heel is longer than that from the little toe to the heel. Although not as flexible as the hand, the foot is singularly adaptable to any number of smooth or irregular surfaces. Heavily padded on all surfaces that contact whatever we walk upon, the foot becomes a surprisingly complex balancing mechanism, where toes perform separately or together as flying buttresses.

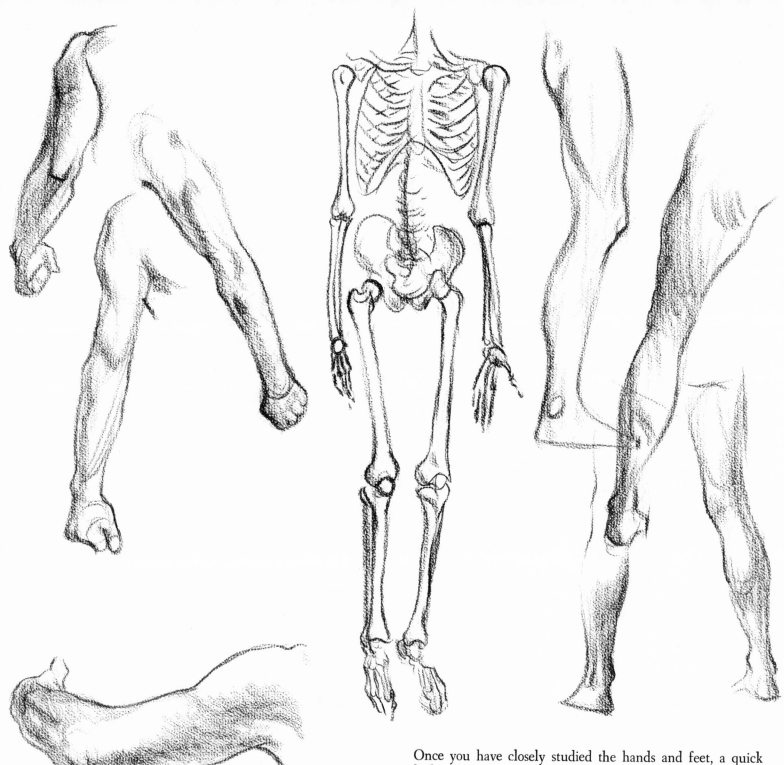

Once you have closely studied the hands and feet, a quick look at how they work in conjunction with arms and legs is in order. After this page, we will be concerned with the figure as a whole.

Try to develop a way of looking at the figure and parts of the figure so that you begin to build up over-all knowledge along with specifics.

The male elbow viewed from the rear has a definite squarish appearance. The deltoid fits smoothly into the biceps. The slant of the calf muscle, inside to outside, is opposed to the slant of the ankle. This system of angles is accented when the weight falls more on one foot than on the other.

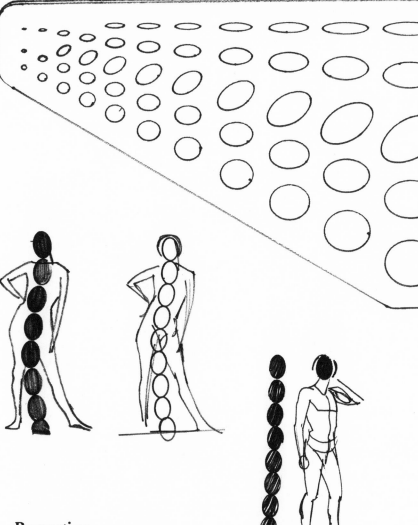

Proportion

Throughout the years that artists have drawn the figure, they have used the human head as a unit of measurement. Most agree that the average adult is about seven and one-half heads tall, but few artists ever draw their figures in that proportion. This is because figures, male or female, drawn to the average proportion of seven and one-half heads, are considerably less appealing to today's viewer than eight-head-high figures. Some of the most adept figure artists, today's top fashion artists, draw their figures nine or more heads tall. This seems to make the clothes more appealing. If we draw our unclothed figures nine or more heads tall, they will look out of drawing (page 49, top right).

During the early stages of learning to draw the figure, using an ellipse template makes it easy to decide, for instance, to put eight heads down for the height of the figure, and then fit the figure into that proportion. I am quite aware that the head shape is not that of a perfect ellipse. It is more egg-shaped. Who cares! We start with an arbitrary shape, sometimes a cube, at other times an egg shape—this is close enough. We'll make all our variations that make the individual head as we go along, but with an ellipse like this, we can quickly proportion our figure in as many heads as we wish.

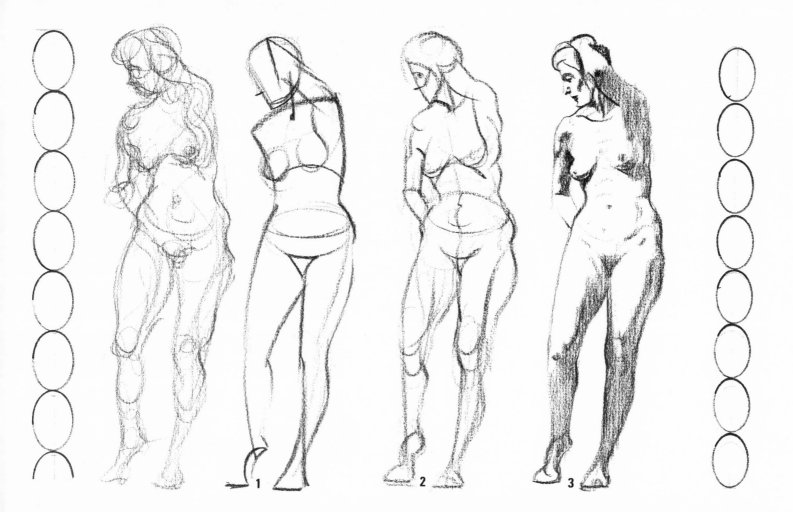

At the left above, I have put down seven and a half heads; on the right, I have put down eight. My first attempt was a scribbling drawing, a seven-and-a-half-head-high figure. Using the same pose, I have taken three steps to an eight-head-high figure. It is hardly discernible in these rough sketches, but I was thinking in these terms as I drew. Either height works. The smaller the head in relation to the rest of the body, the taller the figure will appear.

Using our head measurement, an eight-head figure, or a seven-and-a-half-head figure, we can determine other proportions.

How many heads from the center of the figure to the top? Or bottom? How many heads down to the breasts? How many heads up to the knees?—and so forth.

We can use the head measurement system for horizontal estimating. A man's shoulder width is three heads; a woman's, considerably narrower. A man's hips, two heads; a woman's, two and a half.

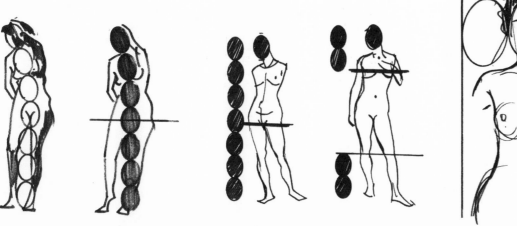

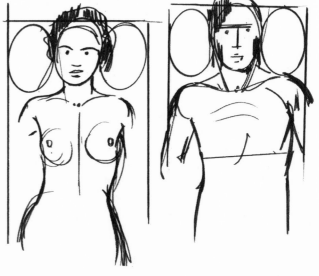

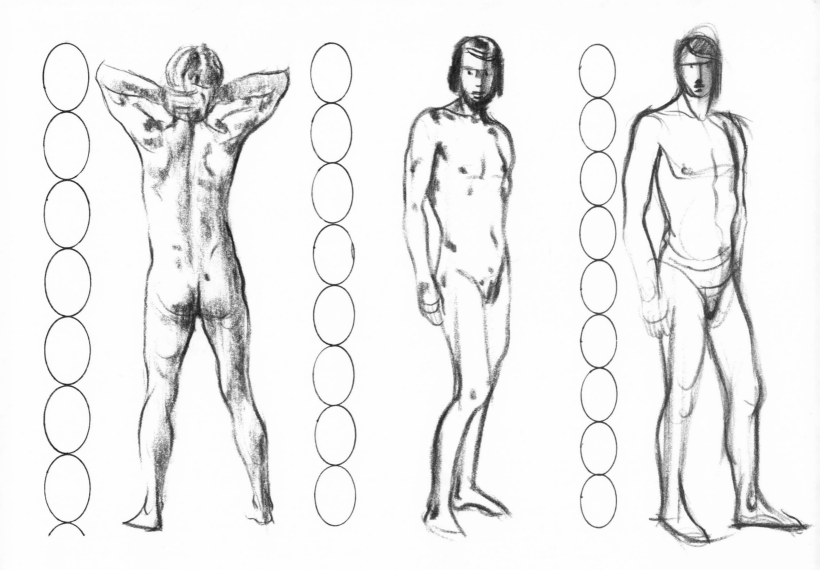

Here we have taken a seven-and-a-half-head male, an eight-head male, and a nine-head male. In determining the head size, consider just the actual bone and muscle structure of the head. It's a good idea again to make the little thumbnail sketches, this time using our template and making figure after figure, little figures, all over the place as I have on pages 48–49, doing it in relation to head sizes.

Using the system of head measurement units, we discover that a child of one is approximately four and a half heads, a child of six, about six heads. An adolescent is normally seven and a half, although considerably slighter in most cases.

As we draw our quick thumbnails of varied-aged people in relation to the head measurement unit, we observe that as the child grows, the center line of his body gradually gets lower and lower. This is a backwards way of saying that the arms and legs grow faster than other parts of the body.

I am about to draw a partial figure, a figure from the waist up. First I determine that the entire figure is going to be eight heads high. I rough out, in outline, an eight-head-high figure. I have indicated four heads on the first drawing. I draw the basic action of the pose and continue into a finished sketch of the partial figure.

One of the most important things in drawing partial figures is that the artist must think about the remainder of the figure, the part that will not appear in the final drawing. Here I have drawn the entire figure to enforce this aspect. Should the artist concentrate on only the section of the figure that he is going to finish, chances are the drawing will be a poor one. If nothing else, he should draw a mini-sketch of the complete operation.

Distortion

The drawings on this page and the next were made from transparencies in projection onto an angled surface with little concern for artistic interpretation.

Using transparencies as material from which to make finished drawings and paintings is popular today, just as photographs, as an aid in drawing, have been increasingly popular since the Impressionists used them a century ago. Much of today's art, commercial, fine, and that in the gray area in between, relies for its detail on any of a number of mechanical devices.

In these pages, I have deliberately stretched figures and distorted head, body, and limbs. I have retained the seven-and-a-half-head ratio but have suggested tallness by means of elongation of the figure much as though the figure were made

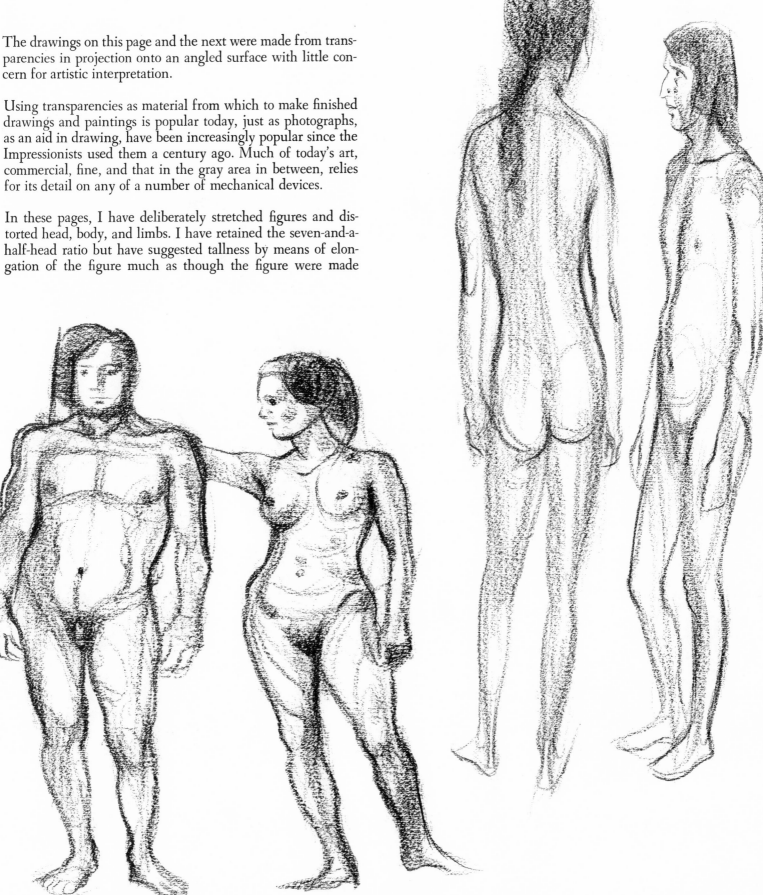

of rubber. Still holding to the seven and a half heads, I have reversed the procedure and made my figures squat and ugly.

While doing this kind of mechanical distortion, I have elongated the figure to appear as though you had an up-front seat in a movie theater.

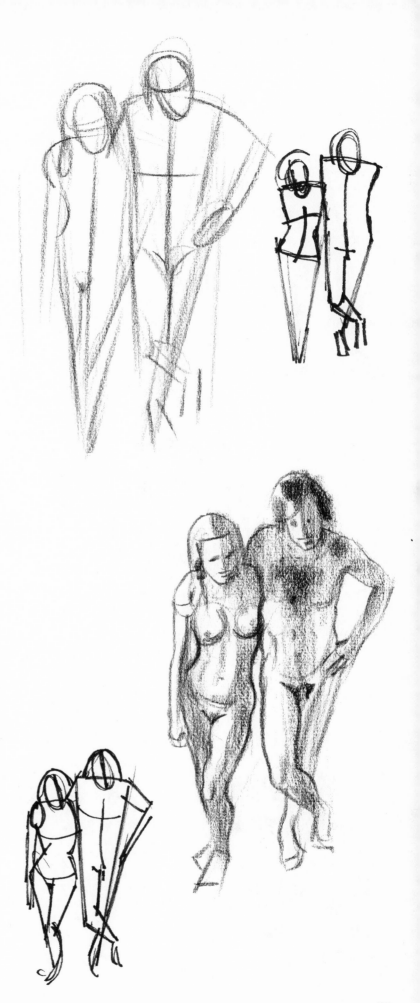

Perspective

In the two larger drawings, I have shown typical procedure leading to a finished drawing. A few thumbnails would be sufficient to begin the student's early thoughts of perspective. Sketching from a position a bit above the model, things about perspective come into play. My vanishing point is, in this case, considerably above the two models. Illustrating this is the small sketch in which perspective lines go into the floor. Ruled lines that converge to a point below the bottom of the page represent the lines of a fireplace and windows behind the posing couple.

On the following page, I have drawn the two models from a vantage point on a balcony. The two, therefore, are in even more acute perspective. Without getting too confusing with vanishing lines going all over the place, I have shown the varied perspective principles that come into play again in this

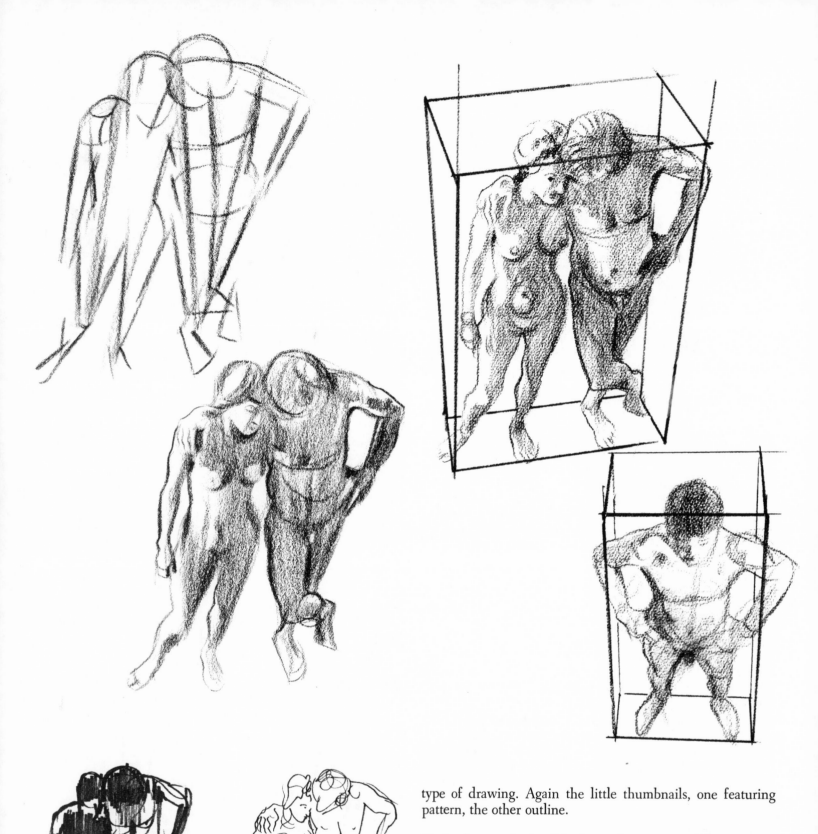

type of drawing. Again the little thumbnails, one featuring pattern, the other outline.

To further emphasize this phase of perspective, I have put my figures into boxes. Continuing the lines that form the boxes will illustrate one-, two-, and three-point perspective.

On pages 53 and 54, I've been looking down; now I will look up at the models. In this case, I suggested to the models that they take the position of Michelangelo's *David*. I didn't discover until sometime later that they had used the wrong hand for the sling and that very likely *David* was a southpaw.

With a low eye level, the lower extremities of my models seem relatively larger. Continue doing the thumbnails. They are easy, they don't take much time, and because they are small, you're inclined to make them more accurate.

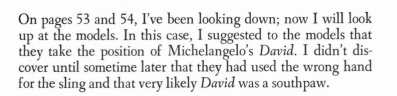

Making a Drawing

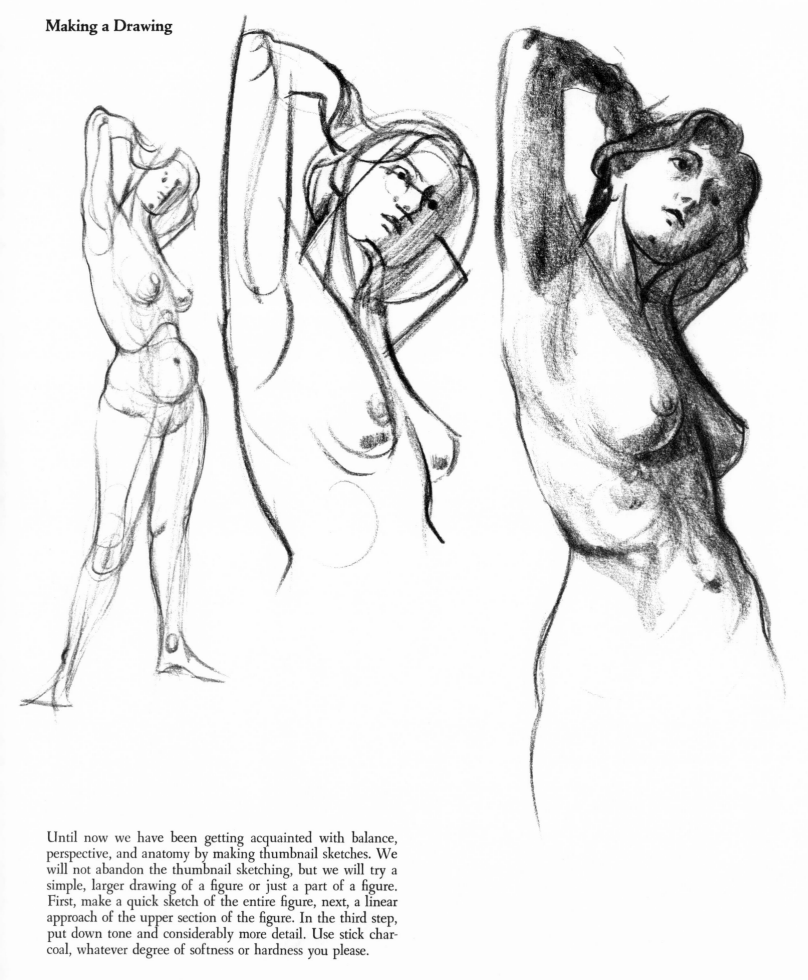

Until now we have been getting acquainted with balance, perspective, and anatomy by making thumbnail sketches. We will not abandon the thumbnail sketching, but we will try a simple, larger drawing of a figure or just a part of a figure. First, make a quick sketch of the entire figure, next, a linear approach of the upper section of the figure. In the third step, put down tone and considerably more detail. Use stick charcoal, whatever degree of softness or hardness you please.

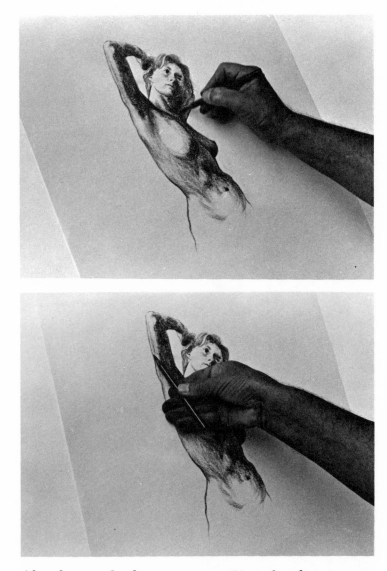

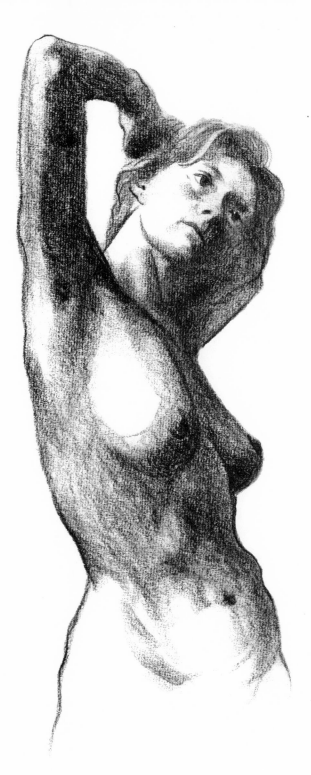

After slapping the drawing on page 56 until nothing remains but a phantom image, make a more finished drawing over this in charcoal pencil. Any rag about the size of a large handkerchief will do for the slapping process. The object is to leave just enough of your original working drawing so that you have a guide for the final drawing. Start with charcoal and continue into charcoal pencil.

The new drawing, done with the aid of all the work that has gone into the original, should be done with greater assurance. It should seem to the audience that the artist knew what he was about. The act of thinking through the original drawing (the one slapped out) should have taught many things. In the final drawing, and in successive drawings, this knowledge will show. At first it might even show too much, but in time you will learn to pick and choose, force and play down, until you are capable of saying what you want to say when you want to say it.

Above is a line sketch of the page 57 drawing. Trace and practice the techniques shown here if no live model is available.

For the finished illustrations you will use a stick of vine charcoal for the entire drawing. Artists' charcoal sticks come in varying degrees of hardness.

Roughly sketch the figure. Take a finger and smudge this while thinking all the time of the construction of the figure. Detail and sharpen edges with the charcoal stick, and continue with the details.

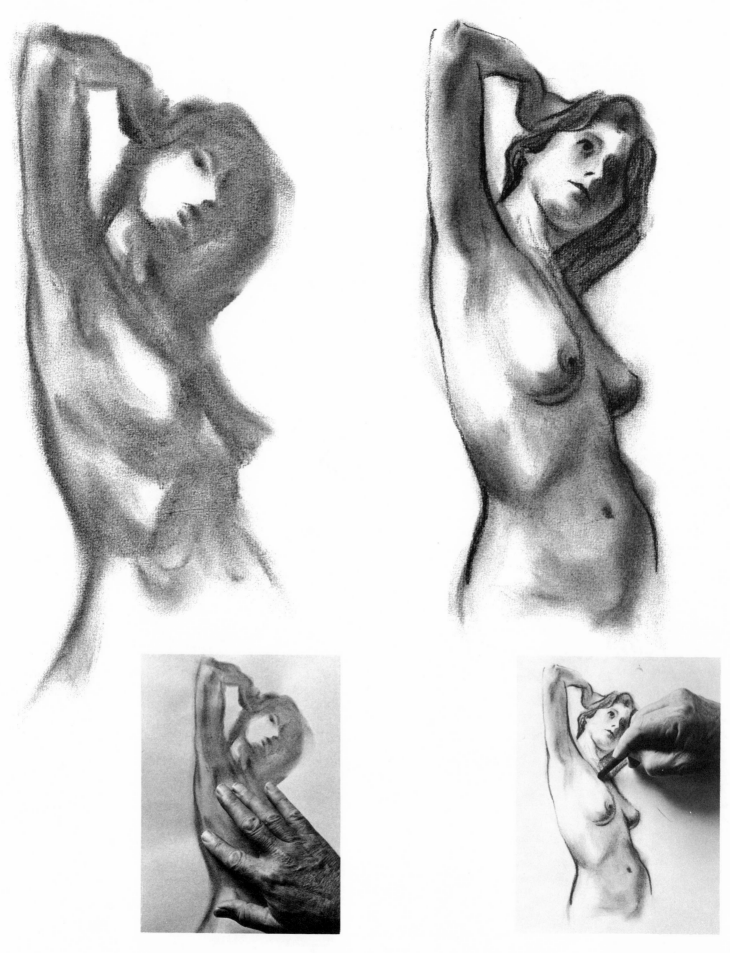

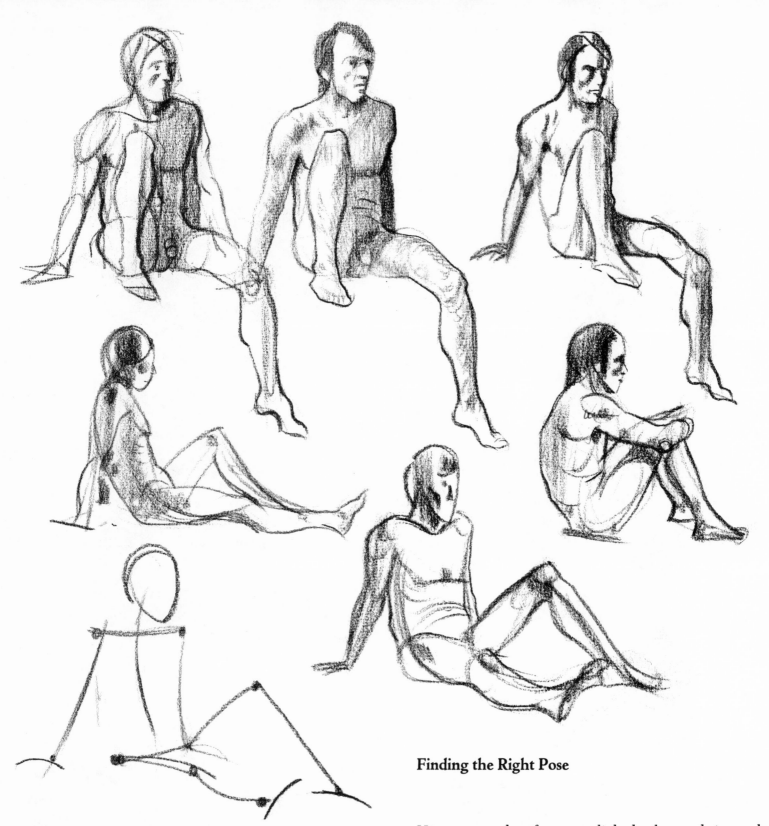

Finding the Right Pose

Here are a number of attempts, little sketches, made in search of a pleasing position for my model. I decide on one, start with a stick figure, bottom left, go to more lineal figures, bottom center, and continue into the large finish shown on page 61.

While drawing the sitting pose I had selected after so many sketches, I observed that the model had a great back for drawing. This back I drew again and again.

60

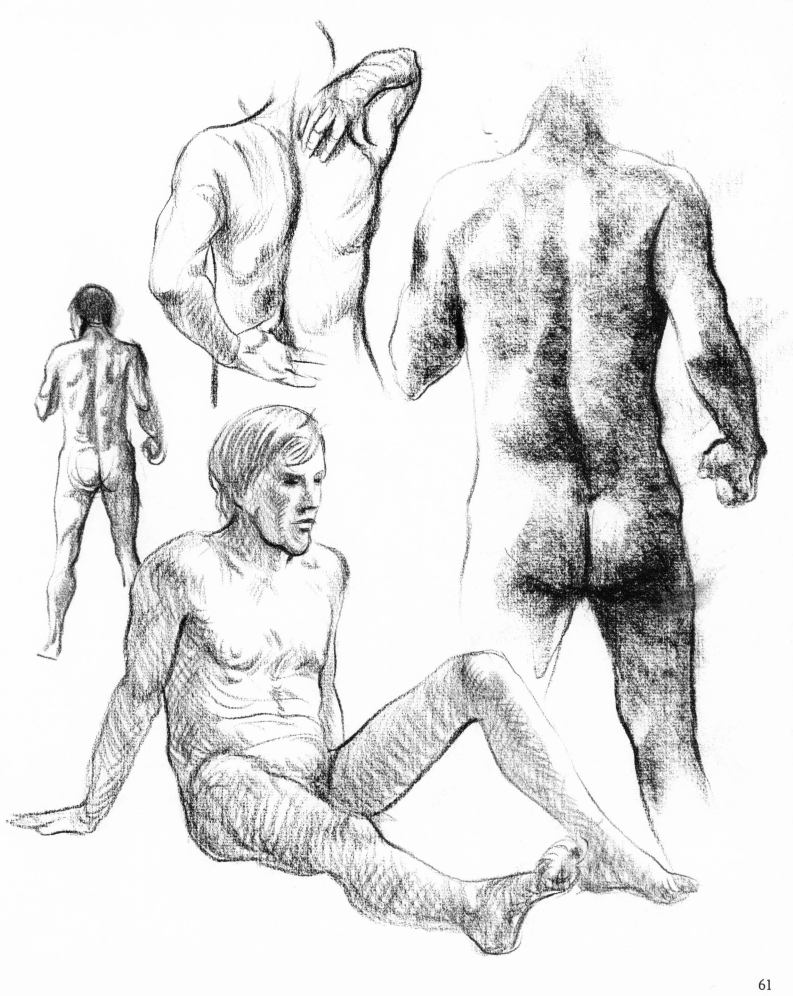

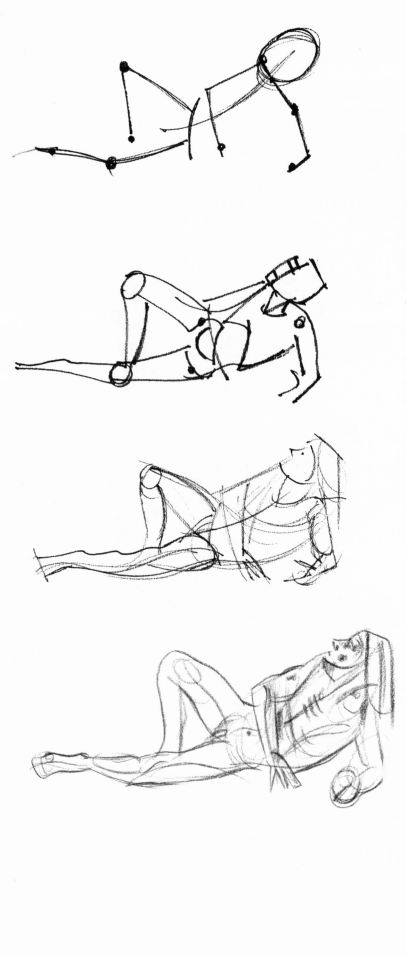

Here I draw a few sketches of the very active male model. First, the stick approach, with little dots to locate the elbows, the ankles, the shoulders, and the knees. Carried a little further, the drawing is blocked out. By the time I am working on the third stage of the figure, the drawing begins to take on action. In the fourth stage I have a complete sketch. In the top photograph, I show the method of using the side of a piece of hard pastel to get a tone. In the bottom photograph, I'm using the corner of the pastel for a line. In the photographs on page 63, I'm making a very simple line sketch with a charcoal pencil. In these last two sketches I've shown the model standing. The model, as can be seen in the photograph, was posing lying down.

Illustrators often draw the model in a simple-to-hold pose only to later show a sketch that makes the model appear in violent action.

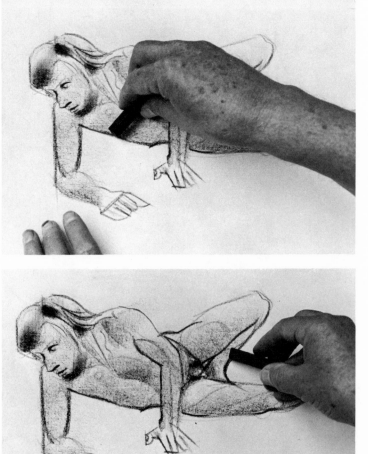

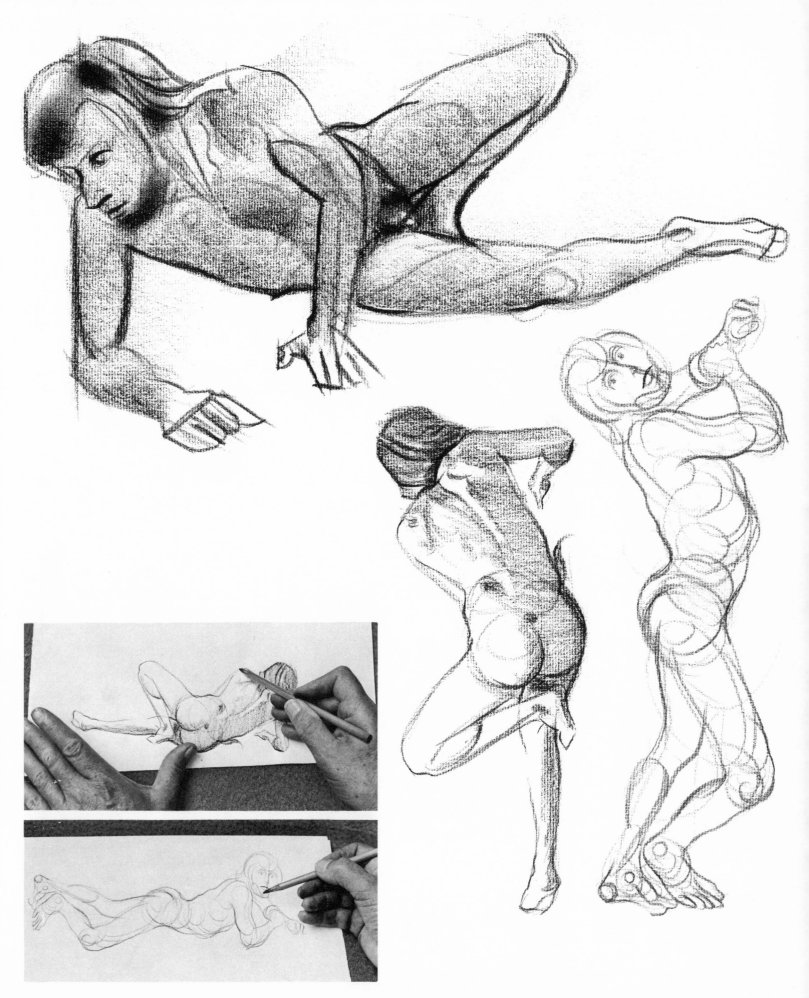

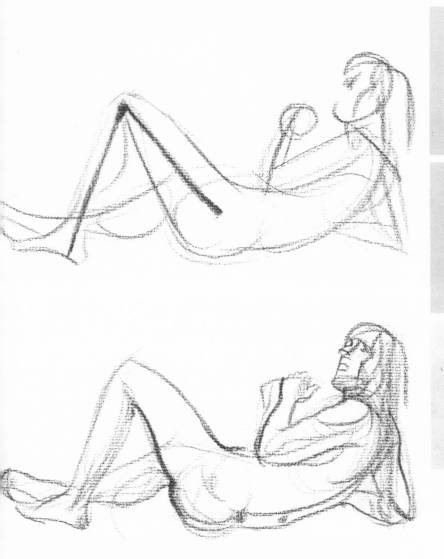

Try a larger, lying down position, starting once more with a "stick" figure and continuing. At times just a change in the size of your practice drawings will help you along the road to becoming a better artist.

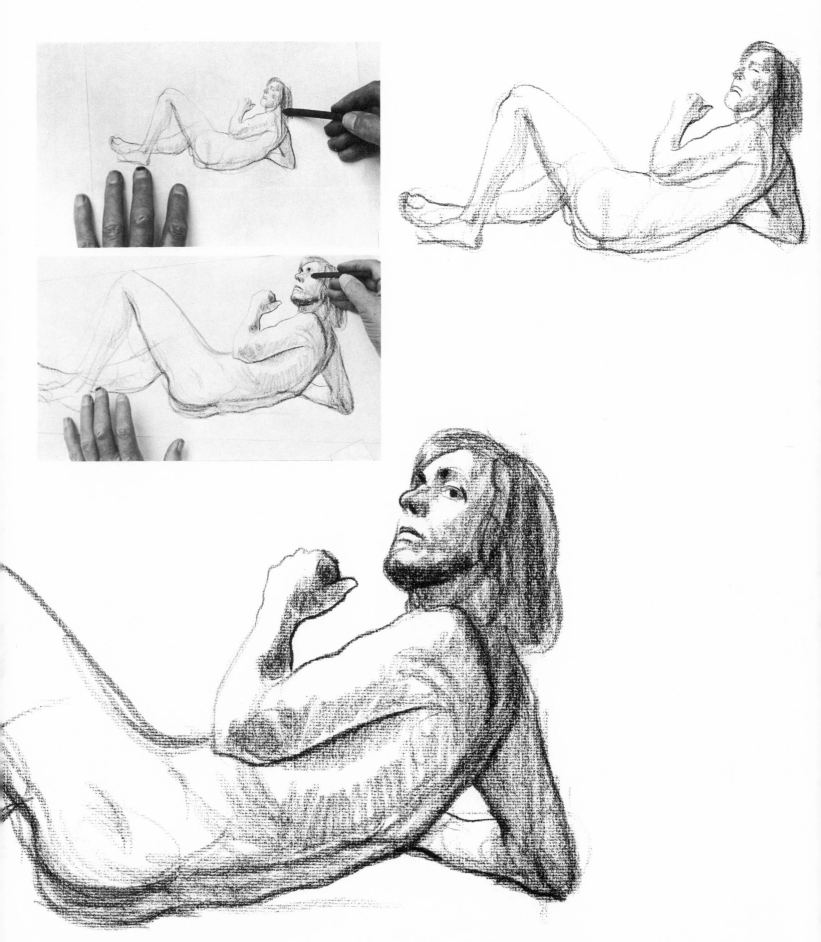

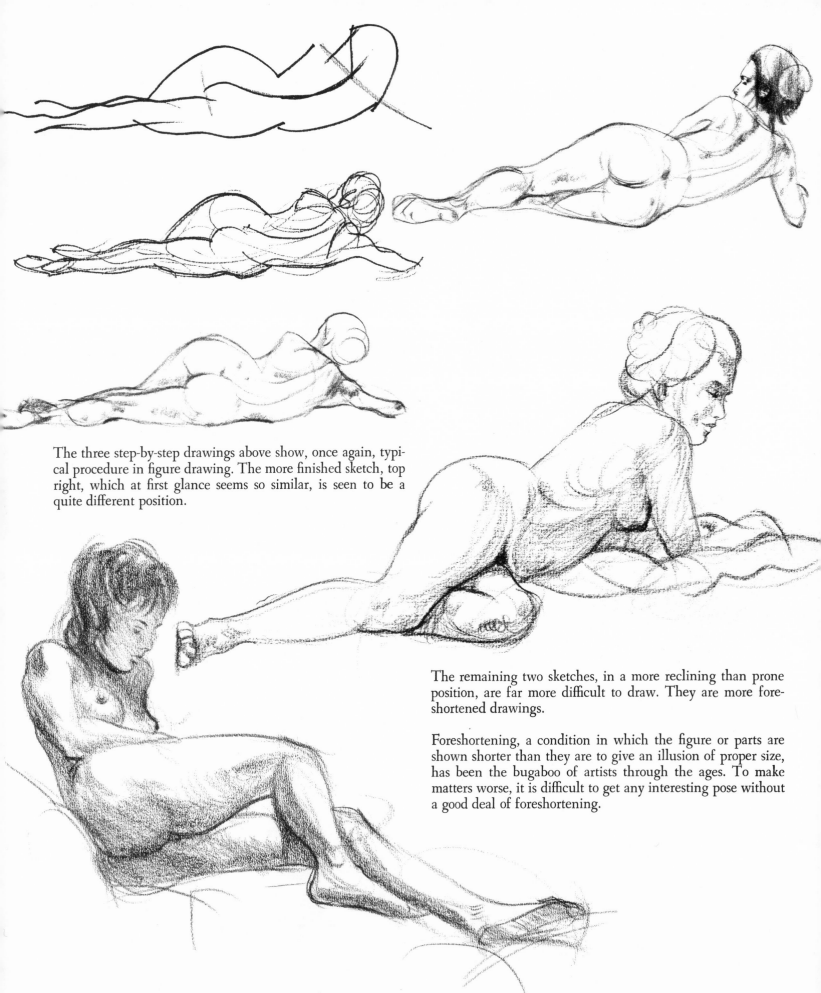

The three step-by-step drawings above show, once again, typical procedure in figure drawing. The more finished sketch, top right, which at first glance seems so similar, is seen to be a quite different position.

The remaining two sketches, in a more reclining than prone position, are far more difficult to draw. They are more foreshortened drawings.

Foreshortening, a condition in which the figure or parts are shown shorter than they are to give an illusion of proper size, has been the bugaboo of artists through the ages. To make matters worse, it is difficult to get any interesting pose without a good deal of foreshortening.

Lying down poses, aside from being a welcome relief for the model, are more at home as wall decorations in today's relatively low-ceilinged homes than drawings of standing or seated figures. At the top of the page are a couple of suggested poses.

The step-by-step procedure illustrated in the remaining three sketches came about when the model was told to rest. Falling asleep, she fell into the best position so far.

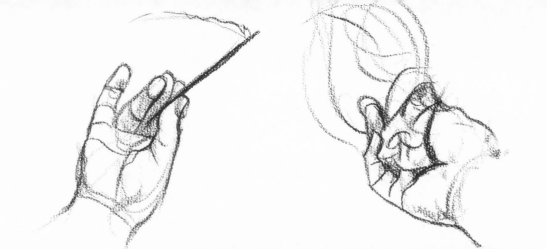

After the fairly long period of sketching reclining figures, try a more sustained drawing. I've picked a pose that is a simple one (if any pose is really simple). With the model facing away, I have no face to draw. With the model posed in a position that demands very little foreshortening, I've avoided the pitfall I mentioned earlier. Across the top of pages 68 and 69, I have drawn five operations that take place in the completion of this drawing. I began the drawing by laying in a gray charcoal tone. I could as well have started directly on white paper and toned the background along with the modeling on the figure.

To return to the five hand sketches, from left to right. The first is of my hand sketching, with a long stick of vine charcoal held very lightly, the overall planning of the drawing in flowing lines. The next indicates thumping out all but a faint image of the early work. The third indicates redrawing with a charcoal pencil or whatever medium you are using. With much of the early mistakes taken care of in the thumped-out charcoal sketch, it's a bit easier to emphasize or eliminate passages. The last two sketches show a smudging with the thumb to get tones, and the use of a kneaded eraser to lighten other sections. The sketches are in no firm order, and the various operations may be repeated time after time, your patience and the strength of the paper being the governing factors.

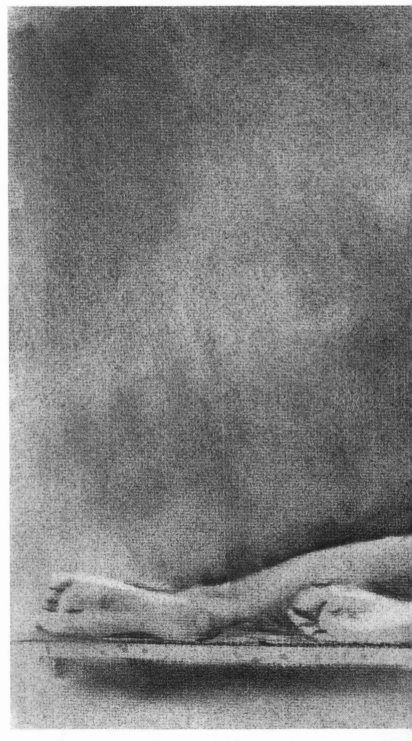

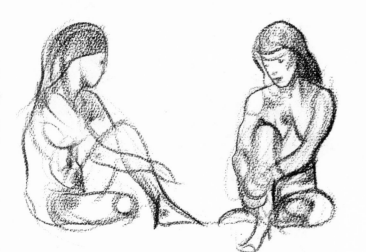

Before deciding on a simple seated position to use in a more sustained drawing, shown in step-by-step procedure on pages 71 through 73, I make a series of sketches as shown above. The one I have selected for completion is the simplest, but any could have been used.

In making your little idea sketches, finish each only to the point where someone can recognize what the model is doing. Go on to the next. As you will remember in our studies of the relaxed skeleton series, it is not at all necessary to have the model, in the exploratory sketches, constantly on the move. The artist can more effectively move around the model. This is especially true in the case where a number of persons have shared the price of the model. Your life-drawing group may be short-lived if you have the model shift positions before one of the other sponsors is ready.

First, on a sheet of charcoal paper (larger than shown in the photograph), I make a gray overall tone in charcoal. I put a chamois cloth around my finger and, after studying the model, take out some of the gray tone. Next I take a piece of charcoal and darken those sections that look dark. Starting at the model's back, I continue into the hair. Finally, I make lineal accents. Although these photographs were of a very, very small facsimile of the large drawing, they give you the idea of how I approached the job. I could as well have done a lot of sketching on tracing paper before I did this. Later I'll do that for one of the other drawings.

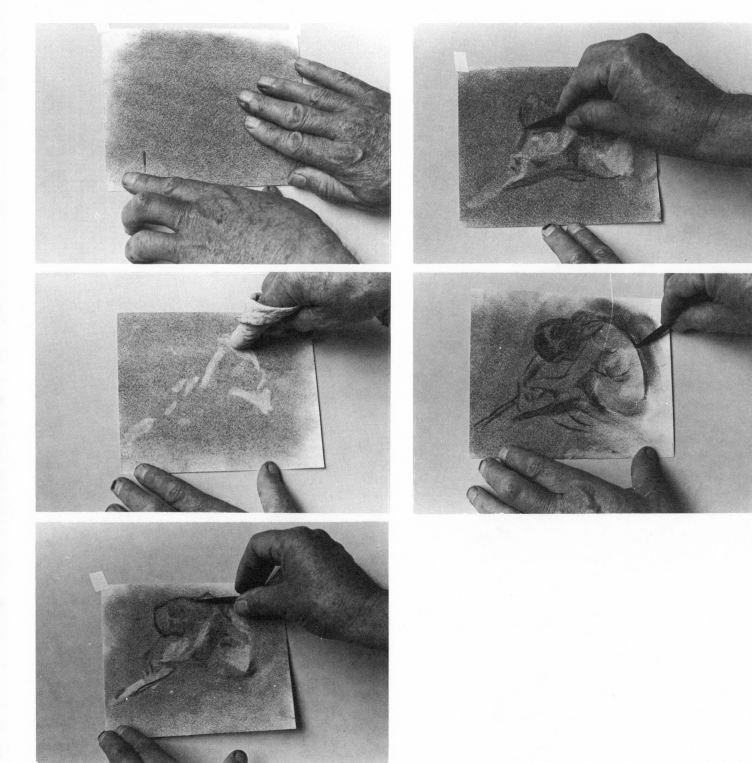

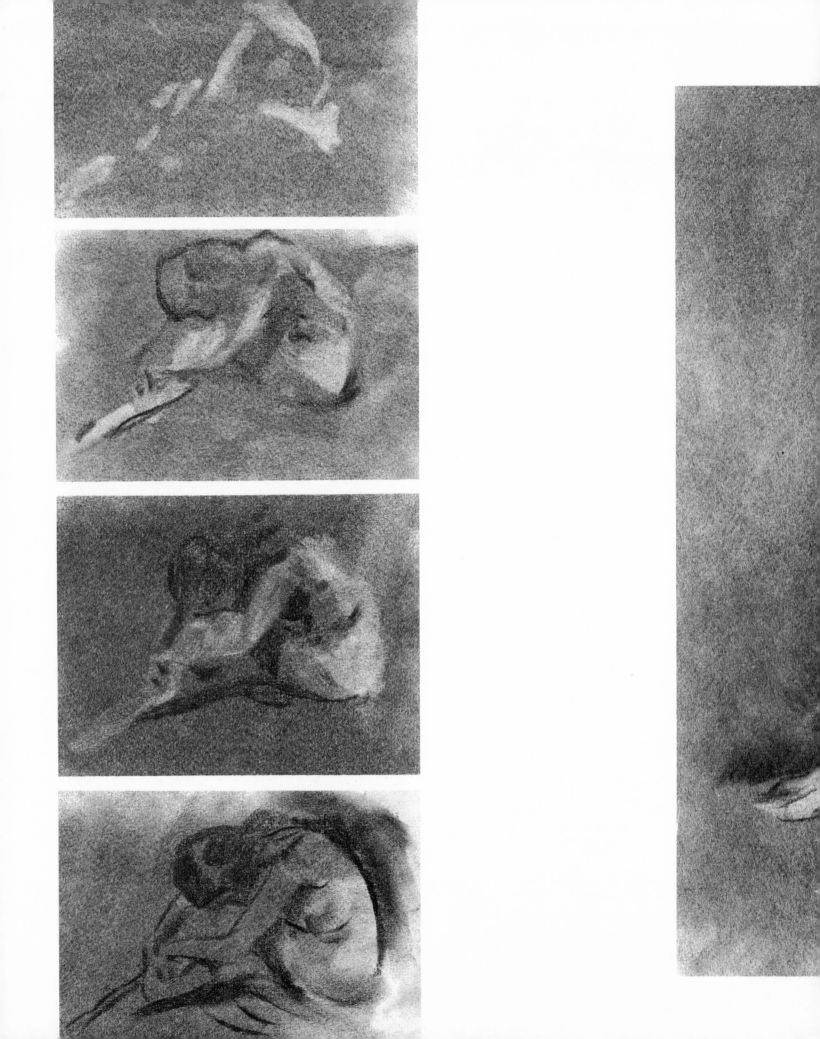

Interaction of Figures

Here, two models pose at one time. In the initial sketching of both models, I concentrated, in mini-sketches, on the action of the poses. The first three step-by-step sketches above are of the woman, the remaining two, of the man.

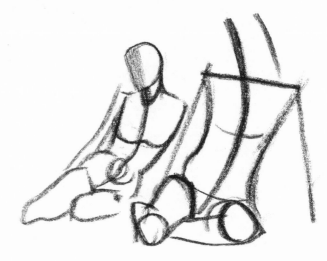

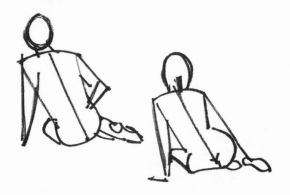

"Action" in this case does not imply that the models were in motion but rather that the flow of line in the drawing suggests a live rather than a dead being, something other than static design. Entire schools of drawing have been founded on this theory of action and counteraction: a line in one direction opposed by one in the opposite. Once the line of action is recognized, it can be accented, forcing the line, so that there is no doubt about the action in the eye of the viewer.

Try even simpler thumbnails. Do a silhouette. In thumbnail sketches, search for an interesting pose. Try a back view. Scribbles and gesture sketches often capture the "feel" of the pose much better than long sustained studies. These preliminary sketches point toward the finished sketch.

74

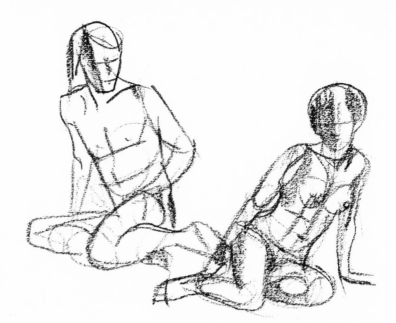

I have drawn the two models in more detail with more thought to construction of the figure. During the time I was drawing them from different vantage points, the models shifted their positions. Had I wished them to remain in a single position, I would have marked in chalk where their bodies touched the floor. Any combination of poses seemed worth carrying into a more sustained sketch, but as I studied the poses, I saw a need to make the design of the two more of a single unit. At the top right, the figures seem to pull apart in composition. Directly below, although I attempted to correct this by having the woman face the man, it was still faulty design. The two sketches of the couple immediately above still seemed to miss, so I continued experimenting. It is interesting to note that this method of multi-starts is routine for the professional . . . unique for the amateur.

As I continued to experiment with additional drawings, I looked back to the early sketches. I wanted to retain what I had liked in my early efforts. In finished drawings, it's easy to lose the liveliness that comes with the initial reaction to the pose.

In time, with a degree of optimism that is a prerequisite for those in the arts, you'll be able to get into your more sustained drawings most of the things you liked about your quick sketches—the freshness and the life.

Once you have learned how to distort and force your drawings so that they say what you want them to, a critic will tell you in detail about a fellow he knows who draws so realistically that you can't tell his work from a photograph. You have arrived if, at this juncture, you can remain calm and say, "That's nice."

As a break from a long stint of working drawings, I take the three sketches on page 76 and do a loose, scribbling rendition, one in which I let the feeling expressed by the models' pose translate through my felt tip onto the paper. I concentrate as I scribble, one line over the next, until I have a lot of lines that can be recognized as figures.

This method of sketching is considerably more fun in execution than the relatively more engineered drawing. Either method of drawing is an excellent method of learning, but gesture sketching, combined with traditional finished drawing, will make the student more proficient in both.

Return to a more sustained drawing, and as you carry the two figures and parts of the two figures to greater completion, think more of the details. What makes one part seem to come toward you? What makes another part recede? In drawing the eye, think of the complete ball shape. Think of what we studied about the hands. Think about all the things that go into making up a figure. By the time you get through, you may have overworked it. Who cares! If nothing else, the last two pages have shown us that there are a lot of composition possibilities in the two seated figures. Start another two seated figures.

In small sketches, draw the man in line and tone. Draw the woman and then the combination (below).

On tracing or other lightweight paper, make your full-size drawing. In the first few lines you will do little more than position your sketch on the paper of the size you have decided (right).

Using these lines as a guide, indicate the joints of the body, the elbows, the knees, the sockets that take the upper arm. In the simplest of forms, draw the rib cages and the pelvic girdles. Refine the shapes of the heads. Make a simple tone interpretation of the pose. Squint your eyes as you view the two. The pattern will be obvious as long as there is but one main light source.

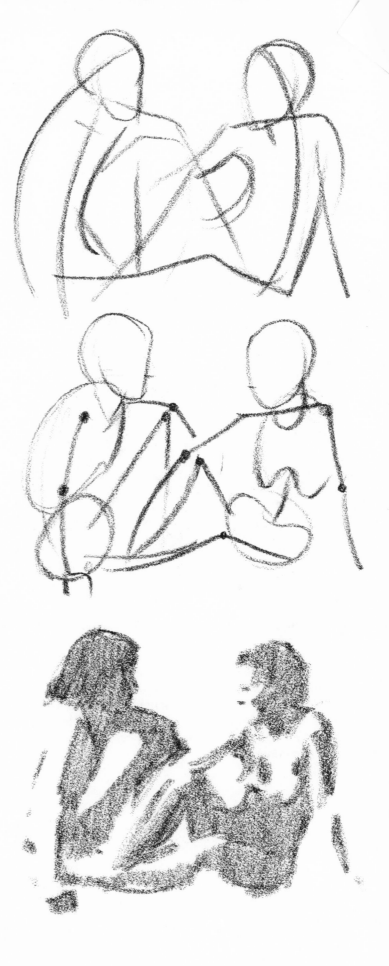

You are about to trace your drawing from the lightweight paper onto the toned paper. If your toned paper is very dark, this will best be done by using white lines. If it is not too dark a toned paper, black lines will be visible. The paper I'm using is not very dark, so black lines will carry. Aside from the tracing paper surface being a responsive surface on which to work, it is translucent enough to see the drawing from the reverse side. We merely cover these lines of the drawing with either black or white pastel and we have a custom-made "carbon" paper.

I made a couple of experimental sketches of heads to see what I'd prefer and then traced my composition onto the toned paper (upper right). This is a re-creation of the process—the actual outline arrived at by tracing is lost as the drawing goes on to the completion. At lower left I have indicated the laying in of white to suggest the major lighted surfaces. Lower right is the drawing with the darks roughly in place. The drawing that you will complete will more likely resemble the large interpretation on page 81.

80

Above is an unfinished sustained drawing of our two models arrived at by following the general procedure outlined on pages 79 and 80. The drawing has been left unfinished so that certain of the lines from the tracing remain visible (the face and left arm of the woman).

1

One of the first rough attempts at composition of the two figures in line and single tone.

2

A move on my part toward my right and I have a composition that seems to give greater emphasis to the woman.

3

In the process I notice that the new composition fits nicely into a 30–60–90 triangle.

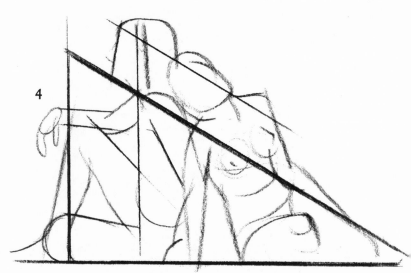

4

The fact that the composition fits into such a definite form is important only as a kind of control in the mechanical part of drawing.

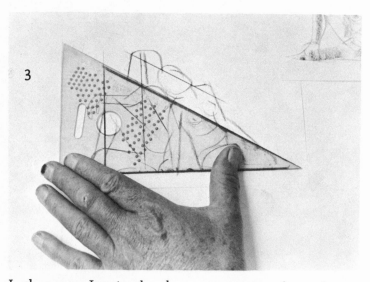

5

As I continue into the construction and detail, I imagine the shape. It could have been any set shape, a rectangle, a square, or a circle.

6

The construction lines are long since gone. The tones, the details, and the drawing are well under control.

Once you have in small sketches what you believe would make a sustained study, use what you have learned to complete a painstaking drawing. Make it a large drawing. Very finished drawings occasionally are a discipline to balance loose, quick sketching. Extremely finished drawing does not preclude simplicity of technique. In the lady on the couch, below, as much or more attention and planning has been given to what has been left out of the drawing as to that which was drawn.

The eye of the viewer creates shapes that the artist implies, but does not outline.

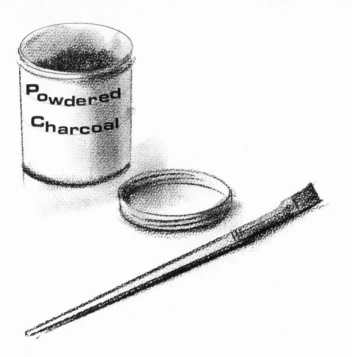

Take but part of the working drawing just completed. You are about to use powdered charcoal as a drawing medium. Powdered charcoal is actually a fine-grained charcoal, made especially for use by sign writers and artists, for tracings, snap-in guide lines, and special effects. You are going to use it as a drawing medium with a brush.

The tracing process here will differ from tracings done previously. Rather than use carbon or material related to carbon paper to make marks on the final surface, you will trace lines by pressing hard with a ball-point pen. If you have used thin paper for your working drawing, the pen will leave incised lines on the surface to be used for the final drawing. Here they will remain almost invisible until you begin toning the paper you are about to use for your drawing of the man.

Dip your brush in powdered charcoal and begin painting your figure. For lighter passages, use a chamois cloth on your finger or an eraser. You can, in short order, obtain interesting results with this procedure. It is a messy, messy job. Don't do it over a white rug.

Alongside are drawings of the operations you will use on a sheet of toned or white charcoal paper. You will follow and refine your tracing with a stick of charcoal. Partially slap out all but a faint image, alternately paint with powdered charcoal, erase, and draw with crayon.

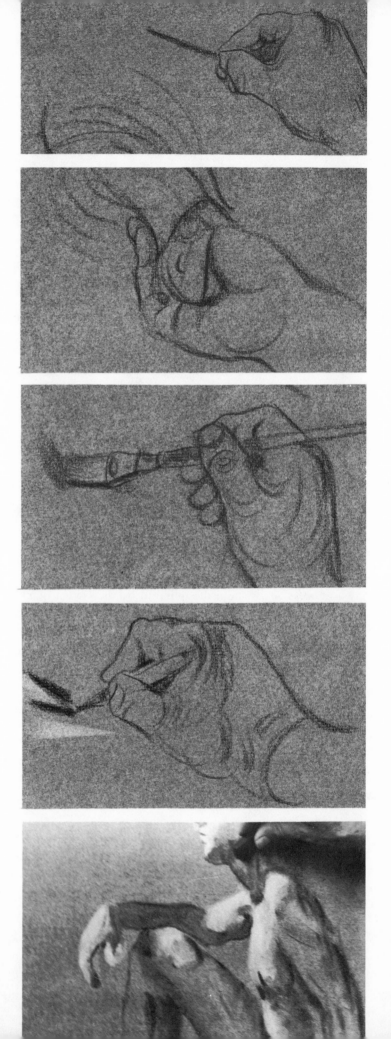

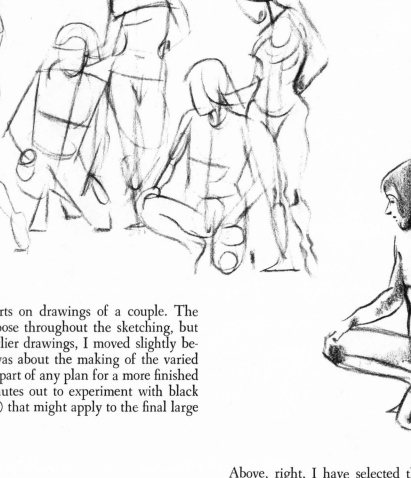

Above are three quick starts on drawings of a couple. The couple remained in their pose throughout the sketching, but as has been the case in earlier drawings, I moved slightly between sketches. While I was about the making of the varied foundation lines that are a part of any plan for a more finished drawing, I took a few minutes out to experiment with black and white patterns (below) that might apply to the final large drawing.

Above, right, I have selected the extreme top left sketch to carry to greater completion. By this time I know how the models appear from a number of angles and can draw with more assurance, from whatever viewpoint I select.

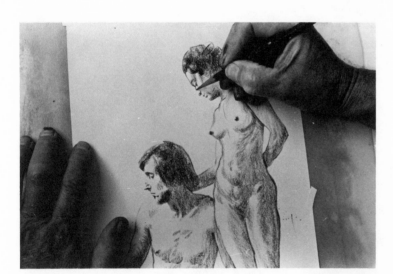

For little reason other than variety, I decide to draw the most straight-on view. Above are three of the steps leading to the drawing on the next page.

On the left are two photos showing the tracing process. This time I used an old sheet of tracing paper with an overall tone of black pastel, well-rubbed and sprayed with fixative, as a substitute for regulation carbon paper. Make this paper yourself, using graphite, charcoal, or pastel on the reverse side. Office carbon paper is sometimes indelible and could wreck your work. Your homemade carbon paper is much better, for the traced lines disappear as you work on your finished drawing. Lay the tracing paper over the sheet intended for the finished drawing with the rubbed side down and the sketch on top. Trace around the outlines of the sketch with a sharp pencil.

Try a two-figure drawing again. To simplify matters, use as one of the two, a sketch you have made for one of the previous exercises. First do a couple of trial sketches using the customary black on white surface approach. Repeat the process, this time using charcoal on toned paper. Trace the drawing on the toned paper and bring it to a lineal, structural stage.

Continue to complete the drawing in charcoal, conté, or whatever suits you. In the photograph below I am using the broad side of a stick of white pastel to create a smooth graded tone on the lighted side of the girl's figure. Use the white sparingly. Think before you put in each light passage. It's the devil to correct.

Catching the Action

To show action in a figure is a difficult problem. To avoid early surrender, it is best to approach the problem in stages. Above and left are three steps each, on two figures. The model has posed so that he appears to be moving.

Here I started with a simple stick figure. I located and indicated important joints with dots. I tried for a line interpretation, at all times working loosely and drawing "through" with sweeping lines. This "following through" method of drawing has been explained before and will be again. Remember a concert pianist's arm and hand motions. These motions correspond to the "drawing through" action of the artist. It may seem an affectation as the artist makes motions far past whatever marks appear on the surface. It is often the difference between excellent and poor in a drawing.

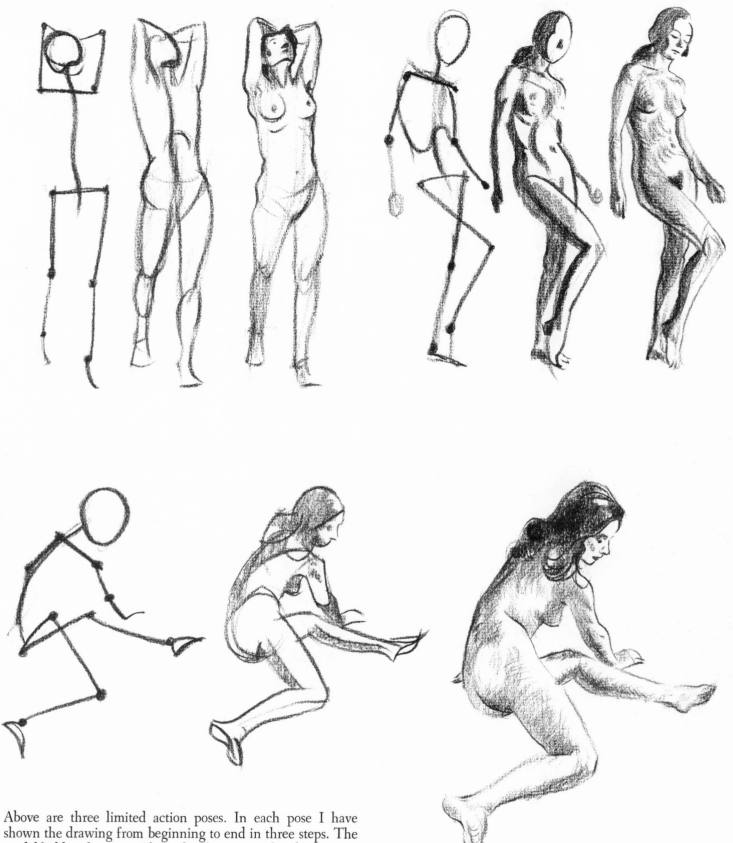

Above are three limited action poses. In each pose I have shown the drawing from beginning to end in three steps. The model held each pose until the sketch was completed.

Another approach to this type of sketching is to have the model hold a position for a limited time, a couple of minutes, then go to another position for a while, and then repeat the procedure. The student can concentrate on sketching a single position but will learn more attempting to do both poses.

Unless you were to follow the photograph route, the actions that you first try to draw would, of necessity, be somewhat limited. Two models working together can get into what appears to be action and hold it long enough for quick impressions. This is great practice. In both of these pages I've started with stick figures and carried through to simplified action drawings. In the final drawings I've eliminated a lot of unnecessary lines. Again, it is a good idea to do a number of little

figures such as the one above at the top right which, unlike the larger step-by-step example, was finished directly and not in stages. The two models kept moving, holding a position for a couple of minutes, then going into another position. In this way, action of the figures somehow gets into action in your drawing. You see what happens to the muscles, what happens to the bones. It's a heck of a good way, this quick sketching method, to learn how to draw. "Practice is the best of all instructors," said Publilius.

Here is a page of quick sketches of people walking. No one is in any extreme action, but he is moving. What happens in walking or running is that the person is constantly catching his balance as he puts one foot in front of the other. It is more difficult to see in a person coming at you or going away. It is good to work on this kind of sketching. It will take a while to produce telling action in your sketches.

Study the figure at games. As mentioned earlier, most sports feature actions repeated again and again. Catch what you can of a specific motion as it happens over and over, each time getting something on paper, until you can carry the entire action to completion. The more you work at it, the better you will get. Be careful not to fall into sloppy drawing habits in which you put down mistakes in observation without thinking.

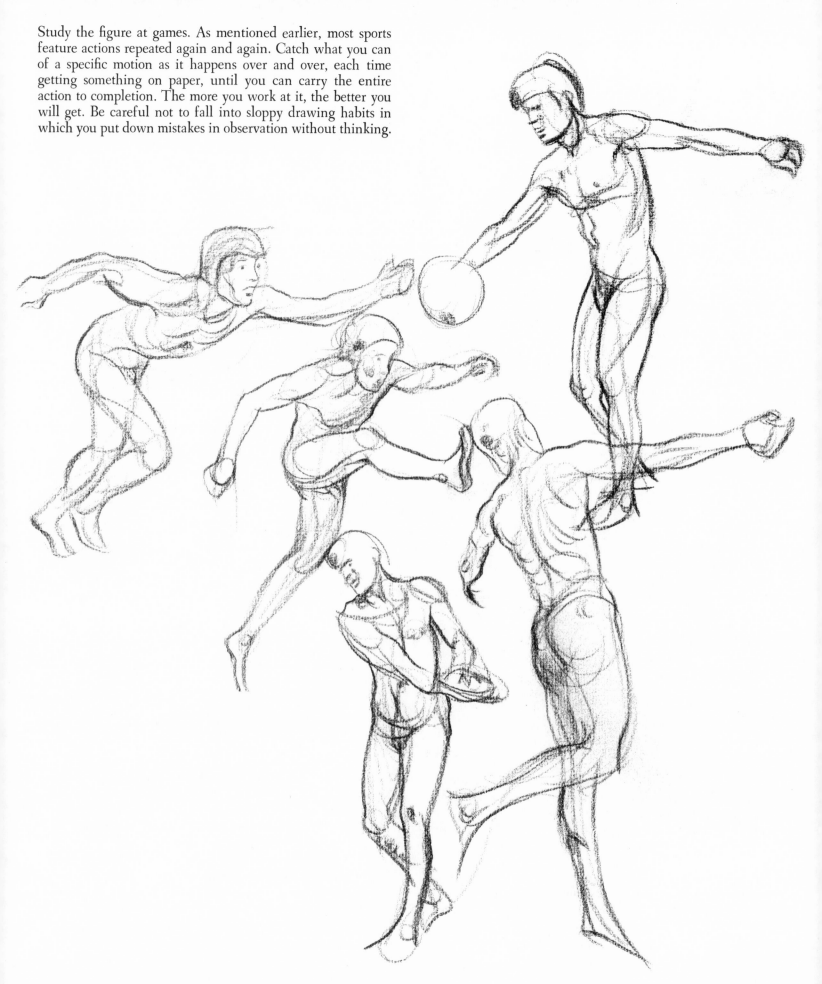

The sketchy half-finished drawings on this page are an approximation of the initial lines that preceded the more finished sketches on page 99. Here we have the first-stage action lines—the lines and thinking that nine times out of ten determine whether your finished drawing will be successful.

Both with and without models, complete page after page of line figure drawings. Don't take time to shade. Try to get a feeling of form by the use of a variation of line. Bring parts forward with relatively darker lines. Note how the lighter lines recede. Draw right through a previous drawing, one right over the next.

If you are on location, at the beach or an event of some sort, you will have little to no control over your models. This fact may frighten you into concentrating harder and working more rapidly. It separates those who want to draw from those who only want to talk about it. The last group sometimes brings out pad and pencil only to give up after the first lines. Those who really want to draw, draw.

A list of reasons why it is impossible to sketch on the spot would go on for pages. Happily there is always some guy or gal who doesn't know about the list and comes up with some good stuff. There is a sketch by Toulouse-Lautrec of a horse and rider; the rider faces backwards. Henri was a teenager when he did it.

I believe that anyone, including all those who have assured me over the past fifty years that they "could not draw a straight line with a ruler," could become a proficient artist were he to make page after page of sketches of life around him.

The models on pages 98–99 consciously held poses for me to sketch. As you examine the drawings, it is not too difficult to recognize this.

Here the same two models lounged around the studio. Later, during a coffee break, they leaned or sat upon the porch railing. Still later, I drew the man as he put on his clothes.

The best thing about sketching at every opportunity is that the artist not only acquires some telling sketches but learns a lot in the bargain. To draw effectively, the artist must have knowledge of his subjects. It follows, then, that through the years the artist builds up a tremendous supply of extraneous facts which, with luck, he can pass off as intelligence.

Taking a selection of the sketches from the preceding page, attempt to see what you can do with outline drawing. To indicate the part of the figure closest to you, draw the lines heavier. Make the lines fainter as the form recedes. Try a few using a same-weight line throughout. Try nervous lines, any manner of line.

Using the same base drawings, make the tonal drawings shown on page 103. The first of these was made with charcoal pencil on rough paper, letting the charcoal tone break into line around the feet and the arms, eliminating other lines altogether. In the standing figures, a tightly rolled piece of paper known as a stump was used to create the tone. In the bottom sketch, vigorous vertical lines were used to create an overall tone. This was contrasted with opposing lines. It has a dashed-off effect that people like today.

At times even the most professional models find themselves returning to trite poses. Amateurs, initially self-conscious—with or without clothes—may appear awkward and stiff. The answer to the problem is the prop. Here, it's a guitar. It developed that the woman of my sketches was a fine musician, and we had an entire series of new poses. In time everyone joined in the act, relaxed while listening to the music. Along with the guitar-playing, we had new poses.

Aside from the full figure step-by-step procedure, make studies of the hands in action, the typical expressions and attitudes of the guitar player and the audience.

The Virgin and Child Adored by the Donors,
after Hans Memling.

The Virgin and the Child Jesus,
after Roger van der Weyden.

Drawing Children

In the work of 15th-century masters van der Weyden and
Memling, for whatever reasons (design concept, a flunked
course in anatomy, or a powerful patron who insisted on a
"little people" interpretation), children were drawn in the
proportions of scaled-down adults. I like to believe that the
artists knew what they were about and preferred babies who
looked that way.

By the time Jacques Louis David (1748–1825) painted *Rape
of the Sabines,* sketched in part at right, considerably more
was known about anatomy and how babies looked. In David's
huge painting all the grown-ups look wooden and posed—the
kids looked relaxed because none of them would hold any
pose and had to be studied in action, I am sure.

It was about the beginning of the 16th century that things took a turn for the better in relation to the drawing of babies, and ever since, our more popular artists have been drawing more believable children.

It's still a difficult problem. A sound approach to even the most finished painting is through the step-by-step procedure shown here.

Drawing children, particularly very young children, can be a frustrating experience. If you can become adept, it can be rewarding. There is an endless supply of child models waiting in the wings, each having a last bit of grooming by parent or grandparent (frequently both). There are few artists who have the combination of super-talent, in-depth knowledge of child psychology, the patience of a cat stalking a field mouse, and other qualities needed to be up to the task. A reminder —heads-high thumbnails will be helpful before proceeding into your sketches of youngsters.

To draw today's child with any degree of success you first use some attention-getting device to hold his interest and, if possible, keep him in your sight. Today's artists favor television. I don't know what artists of long ago used. Other than nativity scenes and airborne cherubs, most childrens' portraits were of the offspring of the rich and powerful. Certainly such parents would have thought of something.

On these pages the youngsters played atop a table. Placing the child on the table limited his area of action.

On pages 110 and 111 is a younger model, happily, a less active one.

Even if you opt to take photographs for future reference, time spent on these quick sketches will help you in your final drawing. The child here is about four and a half heads high.

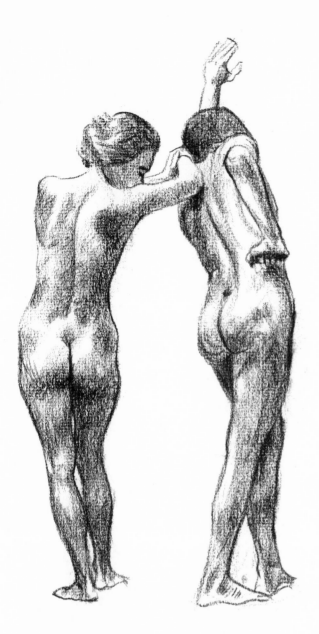

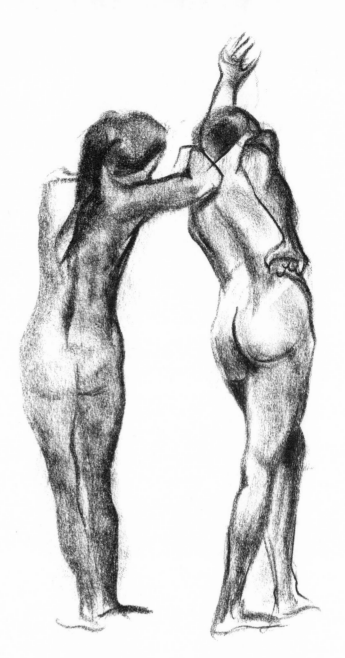

Special Techniques

Here are two similar drawings. The one at top left took some ten times as long to complete as did the one on the right. Each has its place in the business of learning to draw the figure. The kind of drawing on the left allows the student time to concentrate not only on the overall figures but also on details as one relates to the next. It was drawn with a sharpened charcoal pencil, with each line and tone planned. One part of a figure was measured against another part. The pose was such that the models could hold it for ten or more minutes at a time. The sketch on the right was copied from the one on the left. A stick of hard pastel was the medium used. Below the figures are typical lines and tones possible with Nupastel or any of the crayon sticks.

In the drawings directly above, I have shown on the extreme left the approximate first lines that led to the finish. In rapid sketching, the artist almost attacks the drawing surface, hoping all the while that knowledge of the figure will show through the dashing approach. Close examination of the two tones to the right of the first figure will reveal that they could have been the original starting tones of the figure at bottom right. Using this approach makes for drawings that are remarkably free and full of feeling or, in many cases, a wastebasket full of "nice tries."

Sometimes it is good to do an almost-life-size figure. Find a place to work on a wall, using wrapping paper or old newspaper. The stock market page is a simple design background. Use any kind of large paper surface, the cheaper the better. You need several layers of this paper to give you a smooth, resilient surface on which to work, otherwise the least irregularity in the underlying surface will show through. Sometimes, of course, you want the effect of this surface to appear. Working on varied surfaces gives quite interesting effects.

The most usual surface for quick sketching is a pad of news-print. The surface lends itself to the broad sweeping strokes of hard or soft pastel sticks, and it is relatively inexpensive. You can draw one sketch after another and later study all the drawings side by side to see where you are heading.

The business of rapid sketching in this manner can be very exciting. The artist, in many cases, draws lines and tones with so much vigor and emotion that in later review of the work, he often does not recognize it as his own. It is either so much better than he thought himself capable of doing, or considerably worse. Here, using the same approach as on page 113, we have tried not only a full figure, but a partial figure as well.

It is sometimes a worthwhile procedure to do the same pose over and over. Each sketch should take but minutes, with frequent time out for the model to limber up and the artist to finish and think about how things are. During this time between poses, the sound of newsprint being crumpled is heard throughout the studio.

Quick sketching in this manner, in large sweeping tones and lines, with the figure completed in minutes, is a welcome relief from sustained studies.

At the finish of any class or lesson, the room will be almost knee-deep in drawings, some of them unbelievably good. Whether the quick sketches are suitable for framing or for junking, if you have concentrated on what you have been doing, your more sustained studies in the future will be the better for the time spent on these quick drawings.

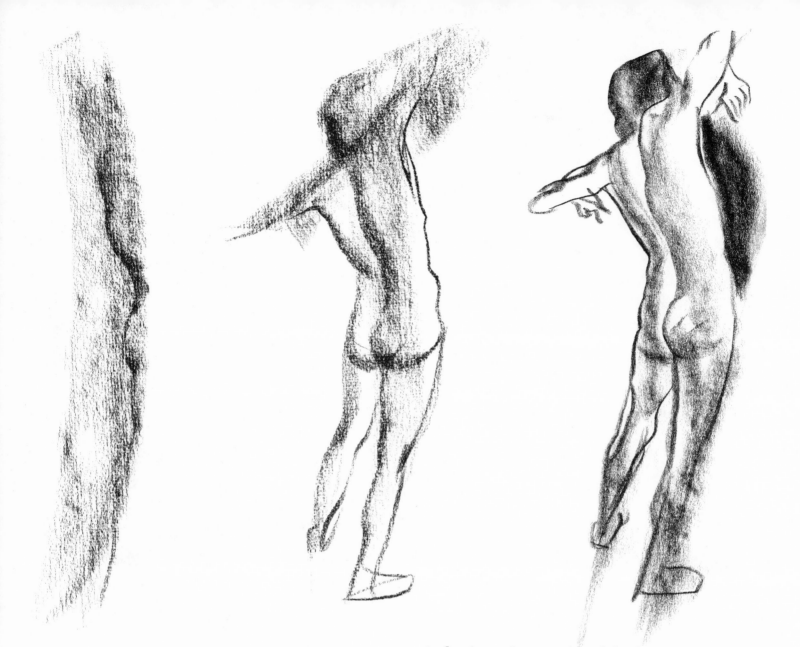

Approaches to this type of rapid sketching are as varied as the artist wishes. The greater the variety the better. Above, I began the sketch of the man by making a broad tone with the side of my pastel stick. I followed this with a graduated tone over the original tone to represent the center line of the man's back. I continued with the drawing until it became clear it was not one to keep, and I started all over again, as shown in the sketch at right. It is difficult to determine in any of the sketches just what the model is doing. The model has a stick held behind his neck over which his arms are draped. Even in explanation, it is difficult to understand why the model is doing what the model is doing.

In the first sketch, things went well from the neck down. In the second, it is even possible that the action, now explained, may be recognizable.

The lesson here is that the details are less important than the execution in a free and feeling manner. In answer to the question, "Why the stick in the first place?", it had worked beautifully in the front view on page 113.

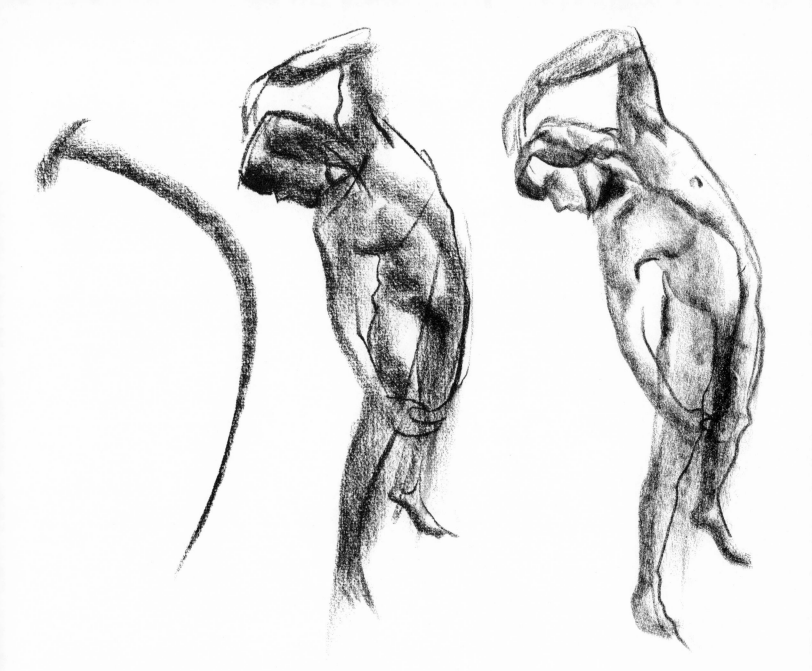

After you have gone through a number of these fast draw-ings, you can use the camera to shoot poses for later study. You can compare your sketches to what will be frozen in a projection. You could, of course, start with the camera, but, as we said in the story of the incident at the Illustrators' Club, the finished work would not be anywhere near as lively. You would learn less and miss the fun, frustration, and excitement of quick sketching.

The camera can be used in a kind of exercise. Take a series of transparencies of the model or models. Project these onto a screen for one or two minutes. Try to draw during the time the transparency is being projected, or study while the picture is in projection and draw when the screen goes blank. This last is a great method to increase your sense of observation. Attempting to remember will force you to look and find the main features. In time you will acquire the habit of omitting meaningless detail.

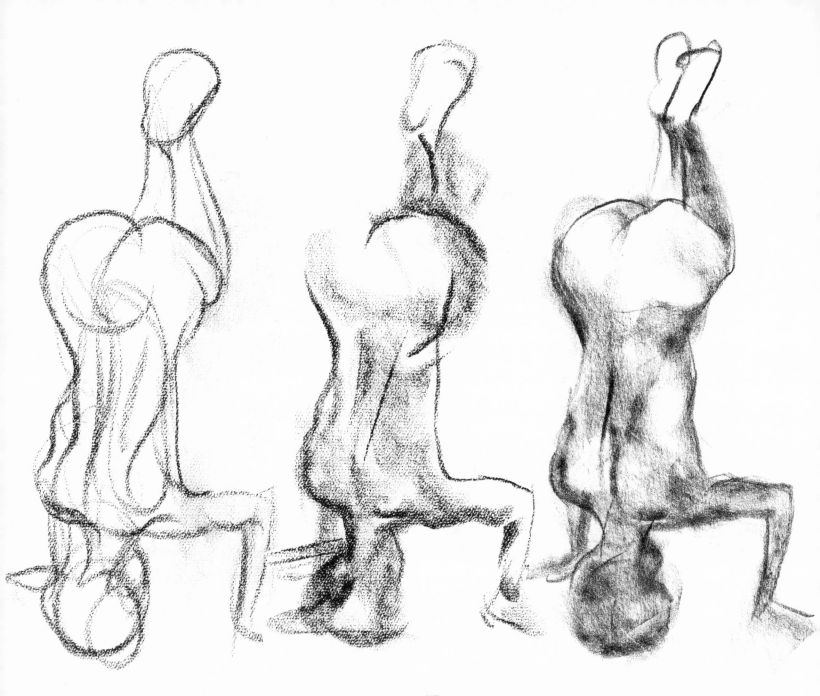

There is no way anyone could maintain this pose for long. The action that the artist tries to capture is continually changing. This type of action is more often captured in drawing than in photography. There have been great action photos, but the type of action that is captured in Duchamp's *Nude Descending a Staircase* and in many of the old masters' sketches, as well as the violent action of the great illustrators of the past, is difficult to top with a camera.

Above are shown three typical steps in quick-sketching the model. In this case she repeated the action a few times. The sketch on the left of page 119 is the final position of the head-stand. The two others are attempts at a slightly different pose from another view.

Rather than sketch while the model is in action, the artist concentrates on the flow of action, and once he has it imprinted on his mind, he attempts to put it on paper.

The sketches directly above are from my book *The Complete Book of Drawing and Painting*. They were drawn in a loose technique with felt-tip pen. The felt-tip pen is great for quick as well as sustained drawing, but so far, I've found no drawings that do not fade in time. If your work is destined for posterity, be careful. Charcoal, India ink, conté, and all the old standbys are safer.

The four smaller drawings to the right were made with a No. 2 pointed brush and India ink. This was a popular style in the 1930's, when these were drawn. The drawings reproduced well in cheap line cuts that could be used in reproduction on the inexpensive paper of the pulps. Young illustrators, in many instances working toward a chance of getting into slick magazines, worked at a frenzied pace. Pay for pulp illustrations was comparatively low and this technique made for speed. After all, you need dip the brush only once in a while. An interesting sidelight on the illlustrators was that in time many of the very best felt at home in the pulps and forgot all about the slicks.

Here, in another sketch lifted from *The Complete Book of Drawing and Painting*, is an illustration using the same materials but another technique. The brush is larger and the approach to the drawing is considerably looser. The little sketches of the '30's on page 120 were first drawn in pencil. The girl above was done directly in brush and ink. I haven't the slightest idea what the pencil is doing in the photograph, which illustrates the manner in which the brush is kept pointed. This technique is a brush wrecker.

The patches above were made with a pen dipped in India ink. There are patterns made of nervous lines, others made with squirrelly lines, still another with dots. They are about as complete a selection of pen marks as you would need for most pen drawings. If, in any one drawing, you combine too many, you get a mess. Here, they don't mean anything. It is just an illustration of types of pen and ink technique.

Ink can be used in other ways. The first photographic illustration shows dipping a toothpick in some India ink. This works quite well. You can make a fairly good line with a toothpick, although it doesn't retain a great deal of ink for long. A Japanese ink block can be used as an ink source. Wet the block and use it much as you did the India ink on the saucer.

The Japanese brush, considerably less expensive than a same-size Russian sable one, is ideal when used along with the Japanese ink block. The many tones and lines that one can achieve are infinite. The three fish shapes, lower right, were made in this fashion.

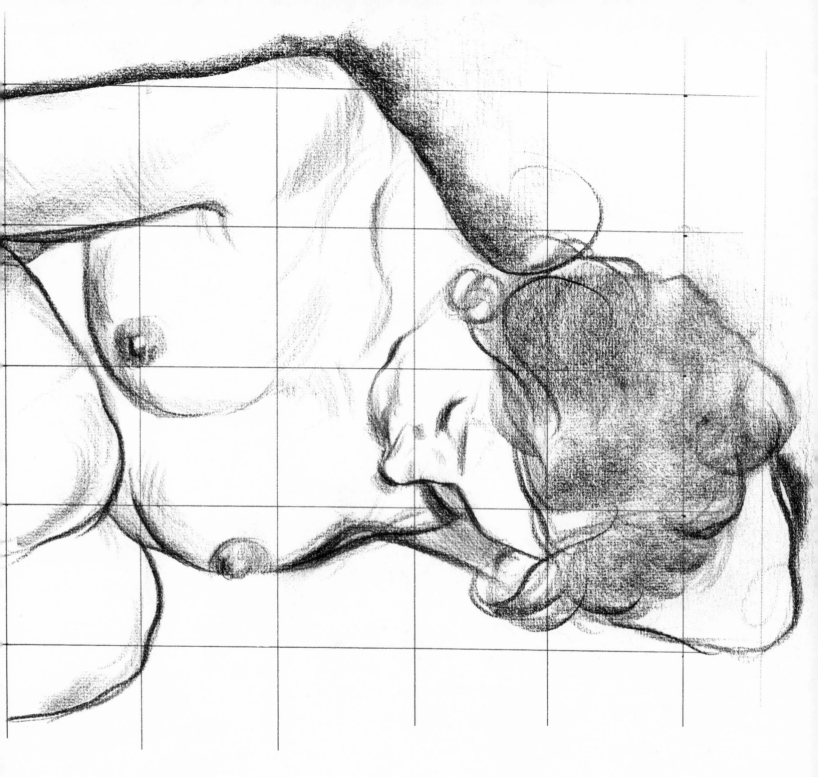

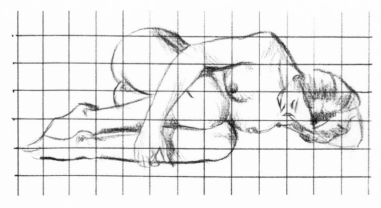

This page shows how to go about squaring off a drawing to enlarge it on another sheet of paper. In the original, the drawing on the bottom was squared off in half-inch segments and enlarged five times.

124

Along with all the quick sketching and sustained studies from models, it is excellent practice to carry a sketchbook and sketch at every opportunity. Most artists agree that this is one of the best habits a student can acquire if he is to become a professional artist. The sketches to the left, made at Shirkston, are a good example of a singularly limitless supply of live, almost life, models.

For figure sketching, there is little better subject matter than people at a beach. There, prudery is gone, along with almost all covering, to be replaced with suntan oil and smiles.

Once I was invited to a supper with Dong Kingman. In deference to his stature as an artist, and adhering to my stand never to play clarinet if Benny Goodman is at the party, I left my sketchbook home. Dong delighted everyone with sketches while he gently advised me to sketch at every opportunity. That was the first and last time I did not sketch when I felt like sketching. Borrowing Kingman's advice, I suggest *you* sketch at every opportunity. If it's figures you wish to draw and no model is handy, go to the beach or the health club.

Sketches at Shirkston Beach, Canada.

PART II / FACES

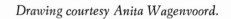

Drawing courtesy Anita Wagenvoord.

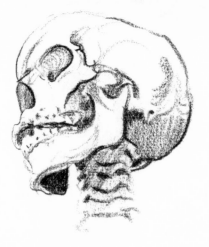

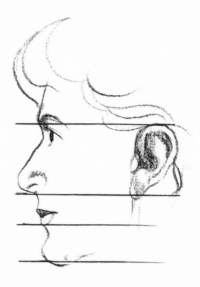

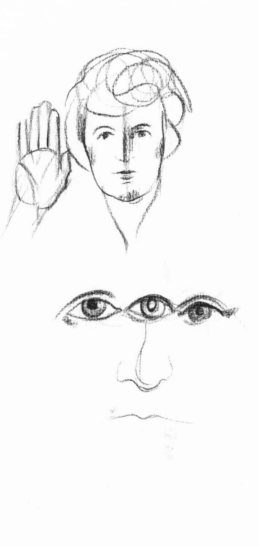

The Structure of the Head

In drawing the head, as in drawing the complete figure, it is the underlying structure that should be of most immediate concern. Despite all the conclusive arguments and examples that prove that to capture a realistic likeness of a person one must take into consideration the structure beneath the surface —despite everything—the amateur portrait artist will start with the eye and carry on in detail from one feature to the next. An argument for the basic-form approach goes something like this. We see a friend in the distance. We cannot tell the special shape of any of his features, much less the color of his eyes. We can, however, recognize him. An older friend gets a new set of teeth. Before he opens his mouth, we know.

Just as we used the head unit of measurement on the complete figure, we may use a few average measurements in the early stages of drawing the head. On page 128 we have the traditional division of the head. In the next few pages we'll go deeper into this division in a few of the many possible positions of the head. For the moment, consider a few traditional relationships to help keep things under control in the early stages of drawing portraits.

First, think of the skull underneath. Note how the ear is aligned with the nose. Compare the size of the face with that of a hand. Note that the distance between the eyes is about the same as the visible eye width. Notice how the neck fits onto the shoulders, higher in the back, lower in the front. A necklace or collar on the model quickly emphasizes this feature. Most artists develop a list of bits of information about the average head. With the classic head in mind, it is simpler to note where the subject being drawn differs.

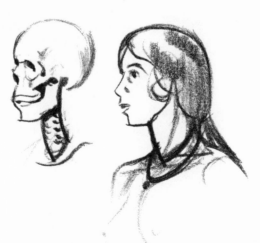

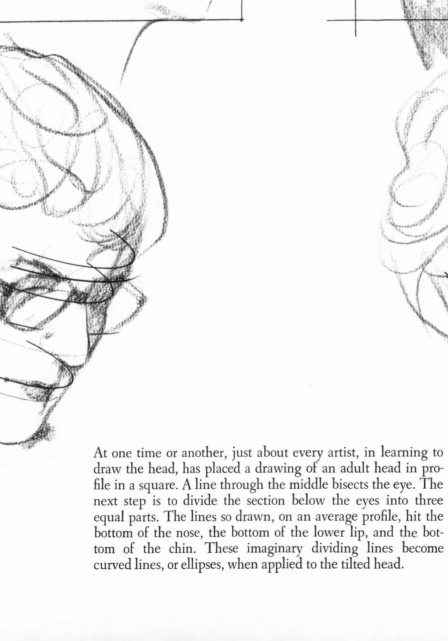

At one time or another, just about every artist, in learning to draw the head, has placed a drawing of an adult head in profile in a square. A line through the middle bisects the eye. The next step is to divide the section below the eyes into three equal parts. The lines so drawn, on an average profile, hit the bottom of the nose, the bottom of the lower lip, and the bottom of the chin. These imaginary dividing lines become curved lines, or ellipses, when applied to the tilted head.

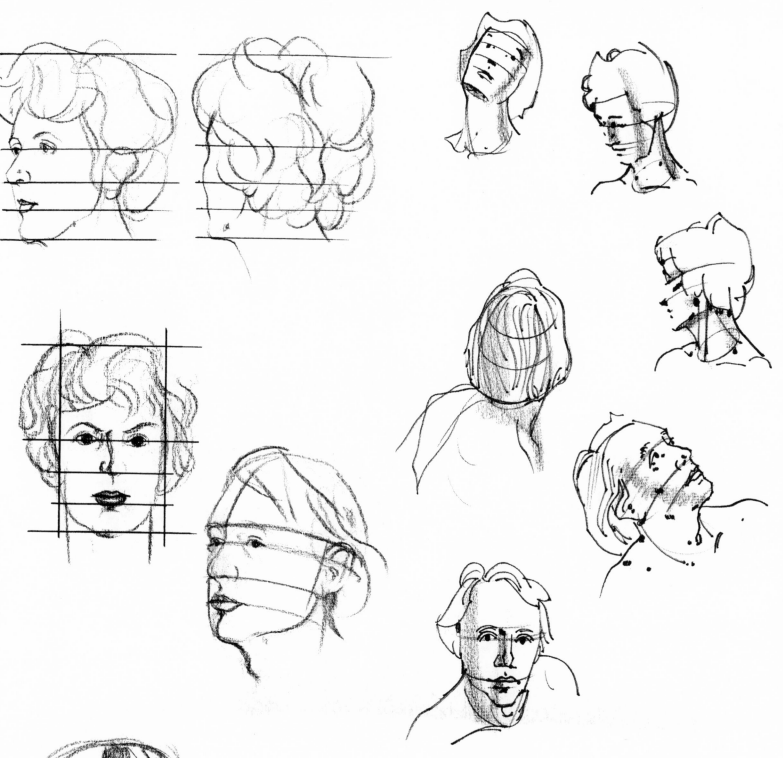

Following Through

Here we have a number of heads in various positions. Draw these heads or any others, and, as you do, draw the line that bisects the head at the eyes. Draw the lines that divide the face at the mouth and the base of the nose. Drawing these lines will get you into the practice of following through in your drawing, which is another way of saying that you don't

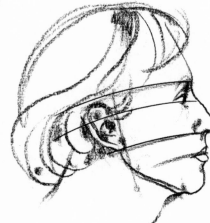

just stop the motion of your stroke where the line stops at the edge of a face. You follow it around, you follow through, you draw the part that can't be seen. If you're doing the neck, although you can only see the front part, carry your stroke around to the back as if you were following a collar around. The forehead, the same way. The two eyes, the same way. You always follow through. Top left, thinking of a head as an egg shape, I have used a light and shadow pattern. I have done the same on lower right. On the others I have just done a touch here and a touch there to indicate shadow, or to indicate something happening in a change of plane. Follow through and the drawing will become more convincing. Most amateurs fall down on this point. They stop the motion of making the line at the point where they can no longer see the line. When you follow the motion through, you get a more convincing drawing.

Male and Female Heads

The male head, in terms of ideal standards, is more rugged, squarer, and generally more angular than the softer, rounder, feminine head. I have made angles on a male head and indicated the neck as being larger. In the female, curved lines replace the male angularity.

An economy of line in drawing either sex is always good but it is more essential in drawing the female head. Unless you are drawing an old, wizened lady (and quite often, even in such instances), it is best to keep all ladies' portraits free of any unnecessary detail.

The neck of a woman is longer, more delicate, and not as wide. A man's neck is almost as wide as his face; the necks of some athletes are even wider. A woman's neck is usually a little narrower than her head, giving the impression of greater length. It isn't long hair that provides a female appearance, especially today when we have as many long-haired males as females. It is the bone and muscle structure.

There is a difference in the eyebrows between the sexes. A man's eyebrows are heavier, straighter, and closer to the eyes. A woman's, even if she hasn't plucked them, are usually more arched.

As a rule, female heads are delicate even while wrinkled with age. Male heads remain more angular and more rugged. As you study the sketches, you see how with even a great economy of line the lower poses are uniquely feminine.

In talks with would-be artists, a frequent question is, "How do you shade the head?" It's a strange question, really. Let's try to make the answer as simple as possible. Make an ellipse with a template.

Put a dark tone on one-third of the ellipse, making it darker toward the center (upper left) and lighter toward the outside. This gives an effect of roundness, since on most things we see, there is some light reflected into the shadow side and our eyes are accustomed to this. When artists draw planets, they don't put in this reflected light because there's usually nothing near enough on the shaded side to reflect into the dark area. You are immediately conscious of it if an orb in a picture is meant to be a planet or a moon because of that lack of reflected light on the shadow side. I'm aware that the lighted part we do see is often reflected light, as in the case of our moon. I refer to the light within the dark area. Most everything that we draw is in a situation where there is some light around and it will be reflected back into the dark area. Of course this isn't always true, but it's true enough to use this as a quick device to get a feeling of three dimensions.

On page 132 I have drawn a series of shaded ellipses and then drawn a head in what is generally the same light. Starting at the upper left and reading to the right, the first spot is an ellipse with light coming from the right. The next sketch is the same shape with features. Continue studying the basic lighted shapes and their counterparts in lighted heads and skulls. My ellipse template allows me a variety of modified egg shapes, narrow for straight-on heads, wider or even compound for side views.

I have taken a different ellipse and drawn a head beside it. It's approximately right. I've done the same thing with a skull. Practice this way. Make the little ellipses and then add features. Make the bottom part of the ellipse smaller, the entire thing more egg-shaped. Continue to do this until you begin to get a feeling for the shape of the head.

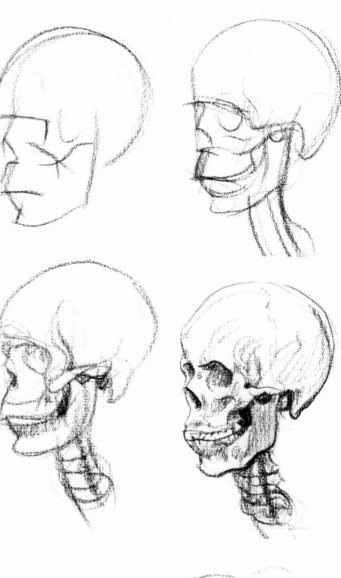

The Inside Story

At the risk of setting the business of drawing the head back a few centuries (which, when you think about it, might not be too bad an idea), I'll begin a study of a simple head by doing a series of step-by-step sketches of the skull. It is not necessary or even advisable to draw the skull each time you draw a face, but if you think in terms of the form, if you know what is going on underneath, the chances are you are going to draw a more convincing face. The only moving part of the skull is the lower jaw. It is not only a moving part but whereas most of the skull stays about the same throughout a lifetime, the lower jaw starts out relatively small and gets larger. It changes considerably. As the child grows into adolescence, adulthood, and finally old age, we have teeth coming in, falling out, and another set replacing these, only to have the second set fall out. In old age the lower jawbone is greatly reduced in size. With the loss of the teeth, the alveolar process—the specialized bone structure that supports the teeth—is absorbed, and the basilar part of the bone alone remains.

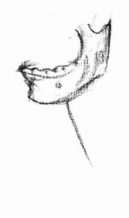

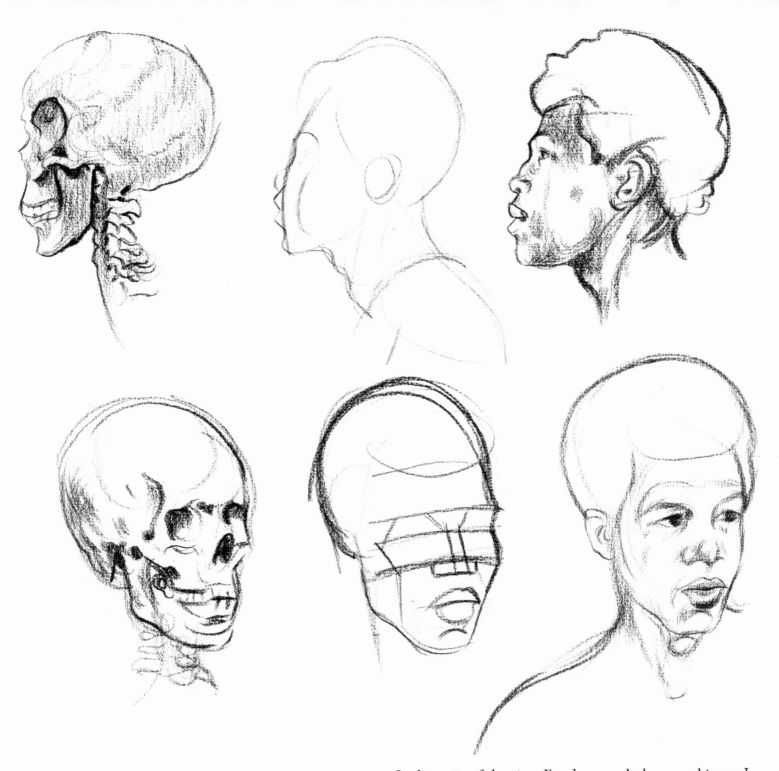

In this series of drawings I've done much the same thing as I have done on the preceding pages. I've taken the skull and drawn a head that more or less would fit. One of the more interesting parts of portrait painting and sketching is that though you constantly, in study, talk about good draftsmanship and realism, when you finally advance into doing a portrait of someone, you will draw anything but a photographic likeness. The more visionary and imaginative you are, as long as you stay within certain bounds, the better. It is altogether possible that by distorting intelligently, you may come closer to the real feeling of likeness than by putting every eyelash in place. A true likeness must stay clear of a photographic rendering.

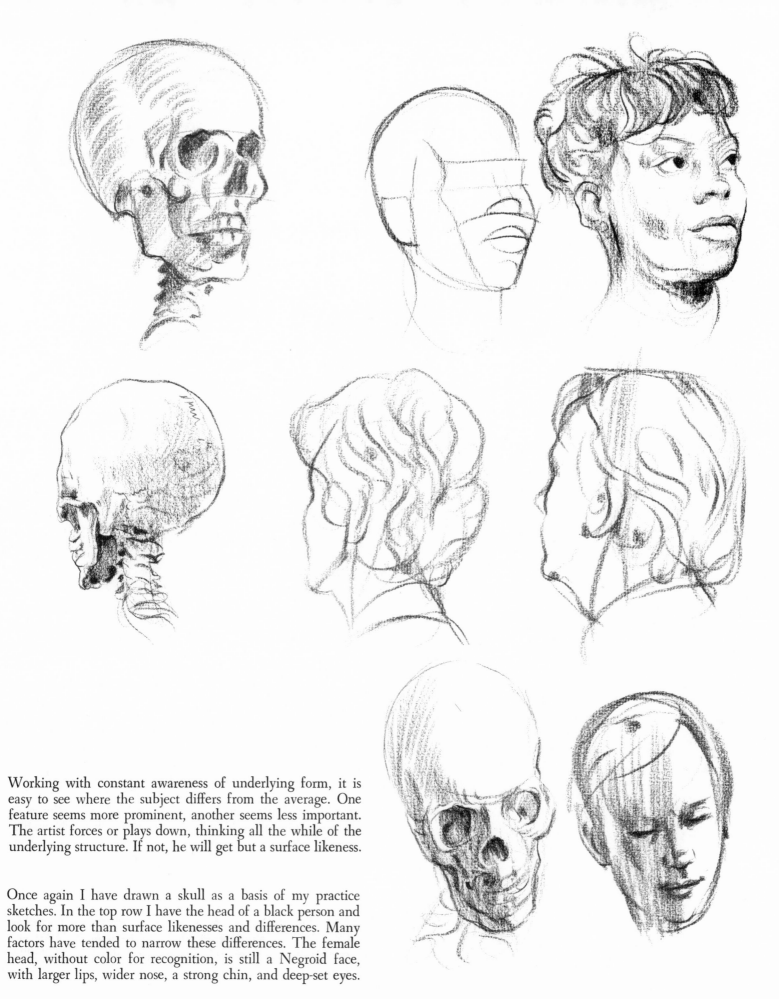

Working with constant awareness of underlying form, it is easy to see where the subject differs from the average. One feature seems more prominent, another seems less important. The artist forces or plays down, thinking all the while of the underlying structure. If not, he will get but a surface likeness.

Once again I have drawn a skull as a basis of my practice sketches. In the top row I have the head of a black person and look for more than surface likenesses and differences. Many factors have tended to narrow these differences. The female head, without color for recognition, is still a Negroid face, with larger lips, wider nose, a strong chin, and deep-set eyes.

135

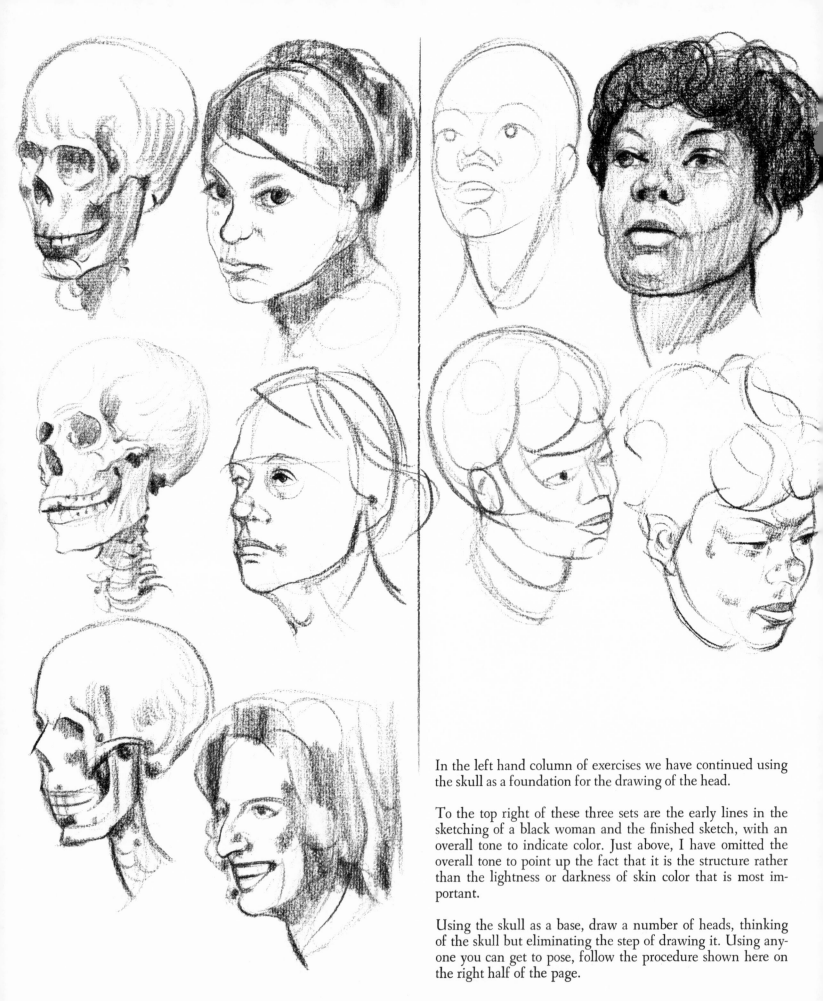

In the left hand column of exercises we have continued using the skull as a foundation for the drawing of the head.

To the top right of these three sets are the early lines in the sketching of a black woman and the finished sketch, with an overall tone to indicate color. Just above, I have omitted the overall tone to point up the fact that it is the structure rather than the lightness or darkness of skin color that is most important.

Using the skull as a base, draw a number of heads, thinking of the skull but eliminating the step of drawing it. Using anyone you can get to pose, follow the procedure shown here on the right half of the page.

The eye is generally considered the single most expressive feature of the face. The eye is ball-shaped and fits into a socket in the skull admirably adapted to accept it. This cavity is so designed that the delicate eyeball is well protected by the rugged frontal bone of the forehead above it and the cheekbone at its base. The eye that we see has a small black-looking center surrounded by an iris that can be any of a number of colors. The white of the eye surrounds this visible area. When you draw the eye, you must be constantly aware of its overall ball shape, with the pupil and iris forming a little raised surface on the eyeball.

The eyelids have a discernible thickness. This we may easily forget and indicate with only a line. The upper lid moves. The lower lid moves nowhere near as much. The eye is always wet. For this reason, it shines and reflects lights. It has a liveliness that other parts of the face don't have. In addition, the lids have lashes which, in many cases, people artificially accentuate. In the inner corner of the eyes, the lids do not unite. They are separated by a narrow, reddish area. The lower lid is generally thinner than the upper.

The mouth is a very active feature of the face. The mouth throughout a person's lifetime owes its changing appearance in part to the underlying structure of the teeth. An old person, sans teeth, looks quite different from what he looked like as a young person.

Think of the upper lip as having three sections and the lower lip, two sections. The upper lip is generally angular in shape, the lower lip, more curved. Of course, lips don't retain this shape during a person's varied moods the way the ear does. The lips move a lot with smiling, laughing, or pouting, and constantly when posing for portraits.

Generally, the upper lip projects above the lower lip. Here, in sketches of lips on cylinders, I have shown the way to think about the drawings of the lips. You seldom draw lips alone, or eyes alone, but it isn't bad for practice. Do this more to become familiar with the features of the face. Concentrating on the drawing of an individual feature, whether it is eye, mouth, nose, or ear, is an easy method of becoming familiar with the likenesses and differences of features of individuals.

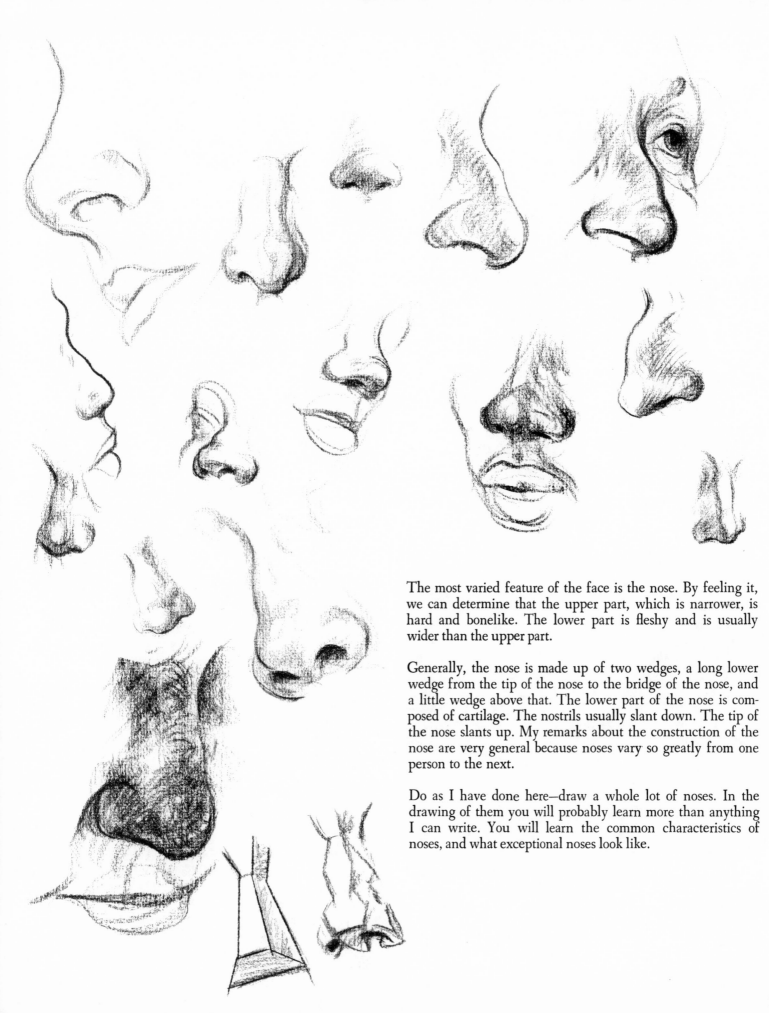

The most varied feature of the face is the nose. By feeling it, we can determine that the upper part, which is narrower, is hard and bonelike. The lower part is fleshy and is usually wider than the upper part.

Generally, the nose is made up of two wedges, a long lower wedge from the tip of the nose to the bridge of the nose, and a little wedge above that. The lower part of the nose is composed of cartilage. The nostrils usually slant down. The tip of the nose slants up. My remarks about the construction of the nose are very general because noses vary so greatly from one person to the next.

Do as I have done here—draw a whole lot of noses. In the drawing of them you will probably learn more than anything I can write. You will learn the common characteristics of noses, and what exceptional noses look like.

139

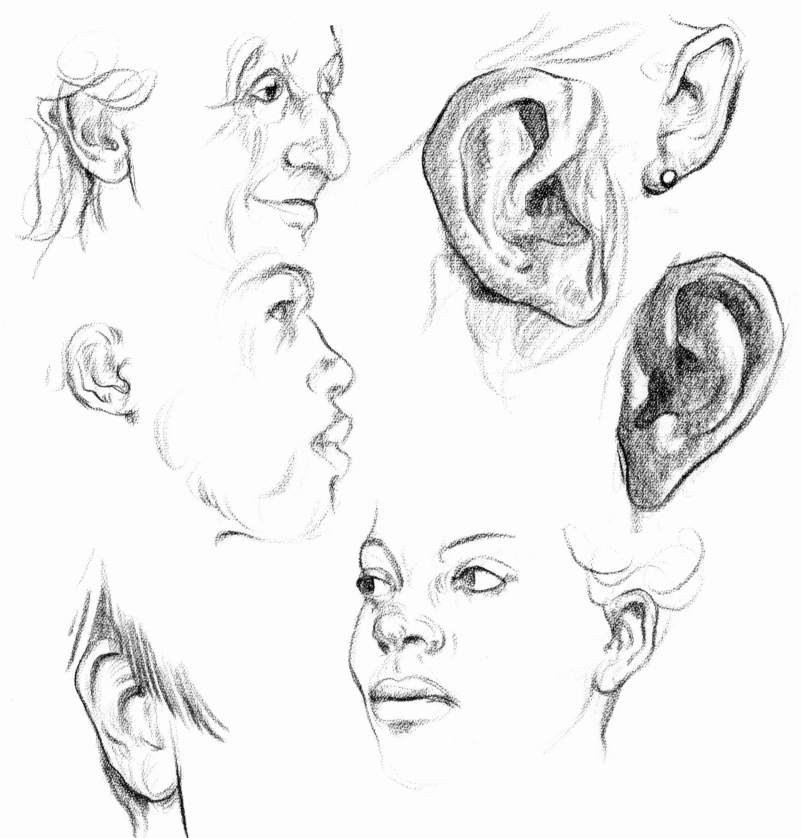

Ears vary greatly in shape and size and are generally considered shell-like in their form. They are mainly composed of cartilage. Looking at an ear from the side, it seems to slant from the top toward the front of the face. In drawing the ears shown here I discovered that a black person's ears are smaller than a white's. Now when I draw, I will keep studying to see if this is generally true or merely that *my* black friends have small ears.

Here I have shown three models to illustrate one way to draw hair. The hair may be mussed, nevertheless the way it grows follows a rigid pattern set by the underlying form. In the top two rows I've drawn this underlying form.

Other things to remember in drawing hair are: Keep it simple. Just a few lines in conjunction with large masses of tone will carry the impression. When you draw, think in terms not only of the visible strands but also of the origins of the hair, even though these roots are not in sight.

Profiles and Portraits

Everything considered, it should be easier to draw a profile than a three-quarter or full face. In drawing the profile I started with an egg shape and added the hair and a few features. I then worked for a little while on the eye and the area around the eye. After that I concentrated on the features in a line study before drawing the three more complete drawings immediately above.

Try a few profiles. They are not too demanding. Do some silhouettes. It would help you in seeing shapes that might otherwise be difficult to define. At all times think of the form, the planes, and the mass. Try a few outline drawings. Keep the work simple. Don't use multiple tones if a single tone will get the story across.

With the same young lady, I try an almost full face starting
with the egg shape. I first quickly indicate an imaginary line
dividing the head in left and right sections. I indicate the
placement of the features.

In the center top drawing I have drawn, in a simple tone, the
overall light and dark pattern. Into this tone I introduced the
features. Structural drawings such as the two large versions of
the head below are excellent practice.

Above, in step-by-step drawings, I have re-created the possible steps leading to the three more complete drawings on page 145. In the top two rows I began with a blocking approach and followed through, emphasizing the roundness and delicacy of the female head.

In the bottom row I began with a simple division of the head, placed the features in their proper relationship one to the next, and experimented with a couple of simple tonal interpretations. There is no single right or wrong procedure. The essential ingredient in all is that of a logical progression of the entire drawing rather than a too early emphasis on any one feature, which, in the case of the amateur, is usually the eye.

Starting with the sketch, top left, and continuing into a more finished one, I stopped to consider whether or not I was heading in the right direction. A few minutes' thought and I could see something amiss. The arm furthest away from me, the young lady's right arm, somehow seemed too important in the composition. The overall pose was one that I liked, so rather than change the position of the model, I changed *my* position, by moving to my right. This brought the model's left arm more directly at me and placed her right arm further away. By the time I had finished the two progressive steps directly above, I knew that this would make a better drawing. The finished drawing appears opposite.

From the very beginning of the three progressive sketches at the top of the page, I was convinced that the drawing was not working. This attitude alone is sufficient to wipe out any artist's efforts. A new pose was started.

This time it looked like I'd have a more interesting drawing. I added the arms and hands, which are most expressive in elderly people. Later I made the study on page 149.

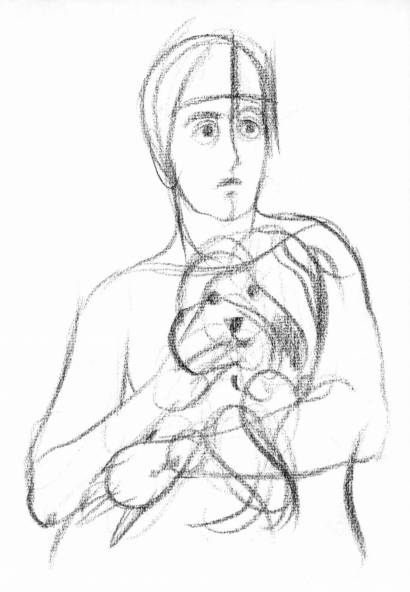

In the very first steps of *Stephanie and Tashi*, I sketched both girl and dog as though they were transparent. As I went from the first stage at top left through the next more structural steps, I added new passages and eliminated earlier ones.

One of the happiest things about drawing portraits is that there is no lack of models. No matter if you are amateur or professional, if you want a model to pose for a portrait, you don't have to look far. One of the subjects here was my daughter, the other, Tashi. Tashi's underlying form is very likely the most "underlying" of any mammal other than that of a musk ox. I had studied her in depth for a sketch I did of her as a puppy in my book *Animals: How to Draw Them*. I had a good idea of the structure beneath her ragamuffin appearance.

Given the prospect of drawing two portraits of a brother and sister, I first tried to capture a typical look of each. While I was about the exploratory sketching, the two got together. It began to appear that I could do a double portrait. After many fits and starts I came up with the drawing on page 153. This was later made into a watercolor painting.

One of the pluses of drawing very young people is that they are generally less critical of the finished job. If they do find fault, it is usually warranted. They accept the more natural pose. They can spot shallowness or depth in drawing, and they offer completely honest judgments.

When you get truly desperate; when you can get no one to pose for you, then—and maybe even before—you do a self-portrait. For a self-portrait with the advantage of a "new" look at yourself, get a few mirrors, three of them . . . do a side view. This is fun because you seldom see yourself in profile. I tried that here, immediately above. I then tried a full face, top, with little luck. I proceeded on a scribble of a full face. Eventually, this beginning was carried to a finished rendition of just the head, next page.

Age and Youth

This is an age-comparison page. In the top row is the grand-mother, lower row, the granddaughter. In both cases I have carried the drawing from the basic form and construction to a drawing in tone. My feeling, in the case of the grandmother, was that the final tone was too involved and should have been simplified. The final drawing of the child was made with rapid vertical strokes in a very loose manner and came off better.

The subjects on page 157 are also all related, the top left and top center, sister and brother, the top right and bottom left, aunts to the brother and sister. Bottom row center is the grandmother, and lower row right is the great-grandmother.

It's good practice to draw subjects of varied ages who are closely related. Try to determine by study what makes an observer say, "You can see the family resemblance."

Above they range in age from one-and-a-half to ninety-two. The youngest, still in the nap stage, has the hair on the back of her head snarled from a recent snooze. At six, the boy has already determined that this posing is sissy stuff.

All of the drawings are sketchy, simple statements. If I succeeded in catching the age differences and the family resemblance, it was because I knew the individuals I was drawing, and I thought about what kind of person each was. I didn't forget to think of all the things I've been writing about —structure, feeling, following through.

Final Drawings

On the next page I have drawn a portrait on black paper in white chalk. It is, for one reason or another, more difficult to get the early stages of the drawing done in white, so I have done the preliminary work in black on white. Starting top left, I carried through until by the time I'd done the sketch at top right, I had decided that the pose was not typical of the subject. I then tried again, with better results. Note the difference in the way the head fits into the body, the more fluid line along the sternomastoid. The model was self-conscious in the first pose, relaxed in the second.

The most effective method of transferring the work of the previous page to the black sheet of charcoal paper is with a sheet of white carbon paper. In this case I made an adaptation of carbon paper by rubbing a white Nupastel over the back of the paper on which I had just made the drawing of the lady. I then traced it onto the black paper, using a hard, red, ball-point pen so that I could see where I had traced, thereby ruining the original drawing. In the bargain, a new drawing had to be redrawn for reproduction in this book.

The preliminary drawings of the lady held out hope for trying a more sustained study. It appears on the last page.